Editors' Notes for *Signs of Life in the USA*

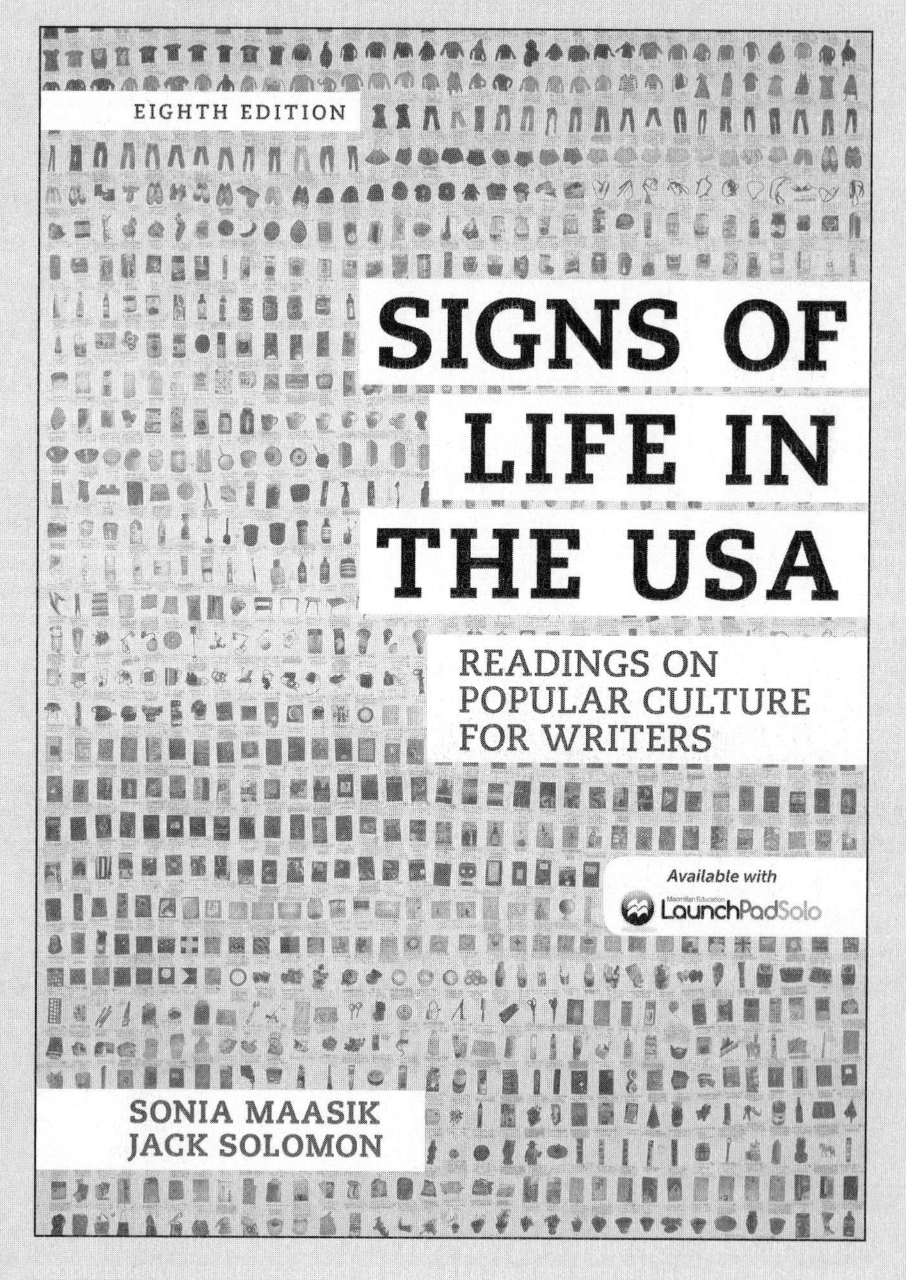

Editors' Notes for

SIGNS OF LIFE IN THE U.S.A.

EIGHTH EDITION

Editors' Notes for

SIGNS OF LIFE IN THE U.S.A.

Readings on Popular Culture for Writers

SONIA MAASIK
University of California, Los Angeles

JACK SOLOMON
California State University, Northridge

Bedford/St. Martin's

Boston ■ New York

9 8 7 6 5 4
f e d c b a

For information, write: Bedford/St. Martin's, 75 Arlington Street, Boston, MA 02116 (617-399-4000)

ISBN 978-1-4576-7086-2

PREFACE

Welcome to our Editors' Notes for using the 8th edition of *Signs of Life in the U.S.A.* We know that before selecting a textbook or even designing a syllabus based on it, most instructors do not read a text cover to cover before planning their course, and they tend to range around in their texts from chapter to chapter, selecting some readings and skipping others. So we've designed this instructor's manual to make it easy for you to use. We suggest possible ways to combine chapters to form a coherent unit and ways to abbreviate chapters, should you not have time to cover all the readings in each chapter. We suggest thematic links that may not always be apparent in the selections' titles but that run throughout *Signs of Life*. And we suggest ways to sequence the readings so your students can build on their experience of addressing other topics.

But the manual doesn't just present organizational plans; it also suggests how you can use *Signs of Life* in the classroom. Perhaps most important, we explain why we've chosen to make a theoretical approach explicit in a reader for composition students and why we've adopted semiotics as that approach. We also anticipate students' responses to the issues raised in *Signs of Life*. This text is based on widespread classroom experience, as we've received ample feedback from instructors across the nation who've used the previous seven editions of *Signs of Life*. Additionally, we've assigned most of the readings ourselves and have used a semiotic approach in teaching students at different levels, from first-years to graduate students. Thus, by identifying which essays are likely to anger or excite students, which selections are relatively difficult or easy to read, which topics are perfect for personal reflection, and so forth, we can help you to devise a class plan that will work for *your* students.

In addition, we suggest activities beyond essay writing that will enhance students' understanding of the issues the text raises. These activities range from journal writing and prewriting exercises to classroom activities such as debates and small group work that encourage lively student involvement. We firmly believe that one of the best things a teacher can do is organize a class such that the students take charge of their own learning. Particularly in a writing class (but also in discipline-specific courses), students need to be active participants in their education. We've designed *Signs of Life* to encourage students to do exactly that. It is based on the premise that students come to college with a high level of expertise in popular culture that you can rely on to generate lively class discussion, inspire a commitment to learning, and create a community of writers.

So what doesn't the manual do? It doesn't "give the answers" to the comprehension and writing/activity questions that follow each selection. While some manuals take instructors through the questions by the hand, we don't do that, for both practical and philosophical reasons. As is appropriate for a composition textbook, there are no readings here that *you* would have difficulty understanding, so we feel no need to outline answers. And even when approaching comprehension questions, you may feel it appropriate for your students to emphasize one angle or another. The writing and activity questions don't have "right" or "wrong" responses, and they don't invite single correct answers. That's not to say that the questions are hard or that some responses might not be stronger than others. And we do provide suggestions for how you can use these questions with your students. It's just that we believe that critical thinking is nurtured if students explore an issue and its nuances, sort out the evidence from several alternative sources that would best support a thesis, and consider what contrary positions might exist. In other words, the questions are intended to encourage students to *think* about a question — to think thoroughly, specifically, and carefully. With that preparation, we feel, students are well on their way to becoming strong academic writers.

A word on the manual's organization is in order. We first provide an overview of using *Signs of Life* in your class, suggesting how to create thematic units, abbreviate chapters, or combine chapters, and giving hints on how to encourage student involvement. We then explain why we've used a semiotics. Next are two essays from instructors who have used *Signs of Life*, offering their advice to teachers new to the book. The bulk of the manual takes you through the readings, suggesting ways to use them in class and anticipating likely student reactions, creating links between selections and chapters, and providing hints on how you can have a lively discussion and assign successful writing topics based on the selections. We hope you find that our suggestions enhance your use of *Signs of Life* in your class!

CONTENTS

Chapter 3. VIDEO DREAMS: Television and Cultural Forms 56

Chapter 4. THE HOLLYWOOD SIGN: The Culture of American Film 64

Chapter 5. THE CLOUD: Semiotics and the New Media 71

Chapter 6. HEROES AND VILLAINS: Encoding Our Conflicts 80

USING POPULAR CULTURE AND SEMIOTICS IN THE COMPOSITION COURSE

Why Popular Culture?

We focus this text on popular culture because we are convinced that students think and write best when they are in command of their subject matter. This command is crucial when students are learning university-level writing strategies, for the novelty of a subject can make students lack confidence as writers or lead them to adopt ineffective writing habits. Sometimes, for instance, students may belabor a summary because they are just learning about it and, essentially, are explaining it to themselves. *Signs of Life* is designed to take advantage of students' literacy in popular culture to generate sharp analysis and insightful interpretations. Now, we don't assume all students are voracious consumers of popular culture in the same way. On the contrary: We assume that our readers will come to the book from a variety of backgrounds, interests, and experiences. The book, and particularly the apparatus, should allow students to share that variety through class and group activities.

In keeping with the increasing academic interest in cultural studies, we also assume an inclusive definition of popular culture. We address topics like advertising—traditionally considered part of popular culture—but also issues such as electronic media that now shape America's social and cultural fabric. This notion of popular culture differs from the one that reigned when we began teaching thirty years ago. We recall a textbook that, as its nod to "popular culture," asked students to compare and contrast a Volkswagen and a Porsche, with no attention to the cars' social or cultural significance. This text used popular culture as an occasion for teaching rhetorical modes; in contrast, *Signs of Life* addresses the way broader issues, such as gender and ethnicity, affect cultural values and ideologies. As a result, we hope that your students will find the readings in *Signs of Life* to be both personally engaging and intellectually stimulating—among the most important ingredients for a successful writing class.

In our experience, students respond to the selections in *Signs of Life* with delight, a little surprise, and great enthusiasm. Indeed, instructors who used the first seven editions report that their students complete reading assignments and come to class eager to discuss the topics. Your students often will be the experts on a subject, knowing more about, say, the latest hit TV show than you do. Some instructors may find that role reversal discomforting. But we encourage you to let your students enjoy the role of expert, for that may well be their first step on the road to enjoying the role of writer.

Some students who enjoy and have some expertise of the minutiae of popular culture may believe that they are already masters of its significance. Most commonly this notion appears as an objection to interpreting popular culture—a complaint that you're "reading too much" into something or that the topic is "merely entertainment." It is useful at such times to concede that, of course, a given television show, movie, or CD *is* entertainment. But the more important question is "What makes it entertaining?" To whit: When masses of Americans, for example, are entertained by reality television programs that feature the humiliation and discomfiture of contestants, or laugh out loud at the latest horrifically violent film, that signifies something about American consciousness. You can connect the enormous amount of *schadenfreude*, hostility, and ironic detachment in contemporary entertainment to a larger cultural system in which social atomization and downright rudeness are increasingly the norm. This response is significant; if students still don't get the point, ask them how they feel when someone blathers loudly on a cell phone during a movie or even in class or in a car, carelessly ignoring or even endangering the well-being of others. Isn't this a sign of a society whose social cohesion is being unraveled, and isn't this unraveling evident in what is considered entertaining?

Why Semiotics?

By making a semiotic approach explicit, we've departed from some textbook conventions. Traditionally, textbook editors assume a neutral stance toward their material, playing the role of objective compiler. Students then read the text, their task being to argue about or analyze it. But we see problems in this formulation of both the editors' and the students' roles. As a comparison of textbooks easily shows, no textbook author is a mere compiler: The choices of what to include or exclude can reveal the author's values and ideologies. This point is hardly new, but our semiotic approach is designed to put it into practice.

Discussed less often is the role of the student. It has long struck us that textbooks invite students to analyze but don't fully explain what that means. There's the old "break up into constituent parts" definition, but that often remains a mystery to students: We're not even sure what it means when applied to complex social issues that don't have distinct "parts." Essentially, analysis often seems like a pure category, with theoretical assumptions and ideological positions unexplored and undefined. But we don't believe there is such a thing as pure analysis, even for students. Indeed, it's likely that, in their discipline-specific courses, students will be asked to use various approaches or theories in their essays. In a sociology class, for instance, students may be asked to perform a Marxist analysis of a social problem; in an economics class, they may be assigned to assess tax-cutting proposals from a supply-side perspective. Being self-conscious about one's point of view is essential to academic writing; we can think of no better place for students to learn that lesson than in a writing class, and the semiotic approach is especially suited to this purpose.

Our own experience has borne out the usefulness of semiotics. As an analytic method, it teaches students to formulate cogent, well-supported interpretations. It emphasizes the examination of assumptions and beliefs and the way language shapes our apprehension of the world. Most students quickly feel comfortable with semiotics: Because one of its goals is to *reveal* interests and ideologies, not to *judge* them, students are less likely to feel that you are peddling a single view on a topic if you adopt a semiotic approach. Semiotics also makes it easier for a class to discuss sensitive or politically charged issues: The goal is not to judge individuals' beliefs, but to locate those beliefs within a social and cultural context.

Using semiotics in a writing class makes sense, too. Much to our delight, students sometimes report that they're covering semiotics in another class. That shouldn't be too surprising, for semiotics also has the benefit of being a cross-disciplinary approach. A wing of critical theory in literature departments, semiotics also has been influential in film and media studies, anthropology, law, psychology, sociology, political science, and even management studies. While we can't guarantee that all students will revisit semiotics in their academic lives, its cross-disciplinary nature makes it suitable for a writing class composed of students who are studying a variety of majors and disciplines. Finally, our students have told us that they enjoy semiotics. In fact, we've had students say that they appreciate learning something entirely *new* in our classes, and what's new extends beyond their writing class to a way of looking at the world.

With that said, we recognize that a semiotic approach may be new to some instructors. We've accordingly designed the book to allow you to be as "semiotic" with your class as you choose. We're delighted if you discuss semiotics with your students, try out semiotic readings in class, and assign them semiotic essay topics. But if you prefer to use the approach with a lighter touch, that's fine, too. Indeed, colleagues have told us that they appreciate the fact that the text does not obligate them to spend a lot of time with semiotics or to involve the class in technical definitions (we've avoided the technical jargon that makes much semiotics research seem turgid). Your class may be content knowing that semiotics means the interpretation of popular culture — and that can be your focus.

Some Background in Semiotics

Students often become intrigued by semiotics, asking about its history and wondering how they can learn about it. We'll anticipate their most common questions here, but don't worry — you don't have to be an expert to answer their questions. Their first question may well be where does the word *semiotics* come from? It might seem unfamiliar because it was coined more than a century ago by Charles Sanders Peirce, who derived it from the Greek word for sign, or meaning, *semeiotikos*. The fact that Peirce, who founded the modern study of semiotics in the late nineteenth century, could adopt an ancient Greek term so readily testifies to the long heritage of reading signs. From Plato and Aristotle to the Stoics, ancient philosophers speculated on the nature of signs; indeed, the Stoic philosophers anticipated contemporary semiotic theory by arguing that the meaning of a sign lies in a concept, not in a thing or referent.

Despite its antiquity, semiotics may be unfamiliar because, unlike linguistics, a regular part of the university curriculum, relatively few colleges have programs or departments in semiotics. Most semiotic study takes place within disciplines such as literary and film studies and anthropology; here, the emphasis tends to be on semiotic theory, which, like any theoretical study, can be technical and forbidding. But just as you don't need to master transformational generative linguistics to decode a sentence, you don't need to master theoretical semiotics to perform semiotic analyses. In fact, we do just that every day, especially in regard to popular culture — and that's why students are perfectly capable of using this approach.

Students really need only a few basic principles to conduct a semiotic analysis. The first is that the meaning of a sign — whether it is a linguistic symbol, an artifact, a belief, or a form of behavior — is found within the *system* to which it belongs, not in some absolute realm of nature or reality. In semiotic terms, the meaning of a linguistic sign, for example, lies in its place within a system of culturally constituted concepts, not in a "real" object to which it refers. Similarly, in popular culture, a BMW gets its significance from its place in the system of automotive status symbols, not from its reference to any sort of concrete referent. It can at once be *associated* with other status symbols (like Land Rovers) and *differentiated* from non-status cars like a Toyota Yaris. Through such differential and associational relations, the meaning of a popular sign is constructed. Your students may insist that BMWs are popular because they're built well, that they refer to some objective measure of quality, but that functional answer fails to account for the many well-built cars that do not carry the status value of a "beamer." Just ask them to compare a BMW to other luxury cars such as a Cadillac. The difference between the cars as they appear within the system is where the meaning lies, in the images that they project, not in the materials with which they are constructed.

In technical terms, the systematic interpretation of a popular sign represents an adaptation of Ferdinand de Saussure's semiological principle that the meaning of a linguistic sign lies in its differences with respect to all the other signs in a linguistic system. Because structural semiology is a formalistic method that tends to ignore history and politics, we have expanded upon Saussure to add both Peircean and Marxist semiotic insights. From Peirce we take the principle that signs are situated in history and that their meanings shift as our knowledge or experience shifts, as well as the principle of *abduction*—or the position that an interpretation seeks the most likely explanation or explanations for a given phenomenon. From Marxism, by way of the writings of Roland Barthes, we take the principle that cultural signs bear ideological weight. Thus, when we speak of the system to which a sign belongs, we refer to historical and ideological (or mythological) systems as well as formal ones. One could say that, in a broad sense, the semiotic method we propose resembles that found in Barthes's *Mythologies* (1957).

Your students are likely to notice that the systematic, or mythological, interpretation of popular cultural signs involves a certain amount of generalization. They may even complain that this constitutes stereotyping. Stereotyping and generalization differ, of course, but it's still best to respond by conceding the point and noting that there are always individual exceptions to the general semiotic rule. Then you can refer to such psychographic phenomena as the Values and Lifestyles System paradigm that James B. Twitchell describes in his selection "What We Are to Advertisers" and that advertisers use to categorize types of consumers. The VALS paradigm blatantly stereotypes consumers, but if it didn't work, marketers wouldn't use it. Indeed, you can ask your students if they recognize their consumer profile in the VALS chart—you may even want to identify to your class where you yourself fit. Of course, in spite of our own self-consciousness about consumer profiling, we find that we fit rather tidily into the VALS paradigm ourselves!

The ability to interpret something by locating it within an overall system is fundamental to any analytic writing, not just the interpretation of popular signs. As a result, teaching your students to see things like cars within their cultural contexts is a step toward helping them to see how, say, understanding Shakespeare in their literature classes requires a knowledge of the cultural system within which his plays appeared. The difference is that in the case of Shakespeare, the cultural system is historically alien to our times and must be learned. In our own time, the systems are well known; they simply need to be made explicit.

This should help you when, after interpreting the status value of something like a BMW, a student says, "Well, isn't all that obvious?" And yes, semiotic analyses of popular culture sometimes may appear obvious, precisely because the systems within which popular signs appear are familiar. But ask your students if the meanings, say, of their clothing styles are obvious to their parents or to someone from a different culture, who may be unaware of the fashion system to which American youth styles belong. The answer is likely to be "Well, no . . ." Then you've made your point!

The key to teaching your students how to conduct semiotic analyses of popular culture is to cue them in to the social environments within which signs appear. In one sense, this involves the teaching of present history, which is rather different from the teaching of "current events," or the larger-than-life events—usually crises—that make headlines. Current events are macrofocused and have relatively little bearing on the conduct of our lives (unless we are in the center of them). In contrast, present history includes everything that we think and do on a day-to-day basis; it is microfocused, and part of semiotics involves bringing to light the details of our everyday lives.

For this reason, a good semiotic interpretation is often *overdetermined*, that is, contains multiple angles on the significance of a popular cultural topic. With such a dense system of signifiers within which any given sign may be situated, one can expect a cultural signifier to have multiple significations. The important move is to be ever mindful of what is going on in the moment that we call present time, and to research, where necessary, those signifiers from the past that are relevant to understanding current signs. A matter of gathering and organizing researchable data, this doesn't require theoretical sophistication.

Thus, one need not be an expert in semiotic theory to be adept at semiotic interpretation. You may have studied semiotics in graduate school or as part of your post-graduate training, and though you may have found stimulating the writings of such semiotic masters as Ferdinand de Saussure, Charles Sanders Peirce, Roland Barthes, Umberto Eco, and Jean Baudrillard, you may still wonder how your composition students will fare in the realm of semiotics. You needn't worry. Just as you can write a syntactically flawless essay without knowing linguistic theory, you can go right to the heart of a cultural sign without bothering with whether Saussure or Peirce should be your guide. The secret is in the system, and that can be your focus.

Responding to Questions about Semiotics

The corollary to our fundamental semiotic precept, that the meaning of a sign can be found in the system to which it belongs, is that meaning is a social construct, not a simple reflection of truth or reality. The systems within which our values and beliefs function are mythologies, not absolute revelations. This semiotic principle — that meaning is mythological (or ideological) in origin — may raise the most challenging of your students' questions, questions that likely will be of two sorts: scientific and moral. Here are some ways to cope with such questions.

Let's start with the scientific objections. We live in an empirical culture that believes in the truth of observation: If you want to get to the heart of something, all you need to do is look at it. European culture was not always like this, of course. In the Middle Ages, for example, the truths of faith were held to be higher than the truths of observation, so Galileo was ordered to retract what he said about what his telescope showed him. But because our society now believes in empirical observation, some students may be shaken by the semiotic suggestion that when we speak of "reality," and of the names we give to our experience of reality, we are speaking of the system of concepts within which we operate, a system that determines what it is possible for us to know.

For the semiotician, our knowledge reflects not ultimate realities, but systems of values that can be called *worldviews* or *cultural myths*. Myths are not legends and stories in the semiotic view; they are value and belief systems that frame the very way we perceive and define reality. From a semiotic perspective, reality is not something waiting passively out there for us to discover: It is the product of our own interpretive decisions. There is always a semiotic frame, a mythology, that mediates between our consciousness and the reality we interpret, and therefore construct, because of that frame. This is one of the most profound and disturbing principles of semiotic understanding — disturbing because it flies in the face of our cultural belief in the sanctity of "objective" knowledge. For that reason, some may find it an obstacle to overcome in learning to think semiotically.

But a little history, read in the light of semiotic understanding, shows that our very belief in scientific objectivity is itself a form of interpretation, not an absolute fact. Fundamentally, your students will probably take a more or less positivistic approach if they object to semiotic principles. Positivism, a nineteenth-century philosophical movement that held that "truth" is revealed through the clear gaze of objective observation, is the ideology of most laypersons today when it comes to scientific interpretation. However, positivism is no longer in force among contemporary scientists. Modern scientists themselves take the position that the "truths" of science are fundamentally interpretations that are themselves made possible by what scientific historian and philosopher Thomas Kuhn called the "paradigms" of "normal science." (Kuhn's book *The Structure of Scientific Revolutions* revolutionized the philosophy of science.) At any given time, according to Kuhn, a scientist pursues the research programs that the state of understanding at the moment permits. In an era of relativity, for example, physicists work within a relativistic paradigm of understanding. If relativity theory is ever overthrown, a new paradigm of understanding will emerge to govern future research. The object of study is reality, but it is the paradigm that determines what the researcher will look for and how it will be interpreted.

The profound effect our cultural mythologies have on the way we view reality are revealed by the varied ways that different cultures regard language itself. In European American culture, for example, the myth holds that the purpose of language is to communicate one's intentions, emotions, or meanings. Language, in short, is regarded as a transparent medium whose primary purpose is to convey information. The natural ground for language is considered to be logic and truth, the projection of objective facts, not persuasion or purpose. Thus, language is considered essentially apolitical, something that ethically cannot be manipulated. We even invent stories to support this mythology when we glorify George Washington, America's most successful politician, as an apolitical man who never told a lie. (Note how the myth stresses his reluctance when drafted as the first president.)

Things were not always thus in Western culture, however. In ancient Athens, wealthy men sent their sons to school primarily to learn the art of rhetoric, which was understood as the art of making political speeches. The Sophists, who ran the schools, specialized in rhetoric—teaching how to manipulate linguistic tropes to achieve one's ends. But it is not the Sophists whom we remember today (except negatively—the word *sophistical* now refers to an argument that can't be trusted, just the way *rhetorical language* today often refers to empty political speech). Rather, we remember Socrates, Plato's teacher, who hated the Sophists—among other objections, he didn't like their habit of accepting tuition fees—and who believed that the purpose of language was to lead one objectively to absolute philosophical truth. Socrates' philosophical predilection to regard language logically and objectively eventually triumphed as the dominant language-mythology of European culture. The Sophists' rhetorically based, political attitude toward language was defeated, and the philosophical view of language as an objective bearer of the truth became the now-invisible (because it is so widely embraced) linguistic myth of Western civilization.

Modern rhetoricians and semioticians, however, can point out just how many rhetorical tricks Plato used in his own writings to attack the rhetoricians of ancient Athens. (We find another irony here: Plato, the first great writer of secular prose in European history, despised and condemned writing as being too prone to trickiness and misinterpretation.) In other words, Western culture's embrace of an antirhetorical mythology of language is based, at least in part, upon some pretty fancy rhetoric. Plato, after all, got his way, which is what persuasive argumentation is meant to do.

Next you might also find a moral objection to semiotics. Some students may worry that the approach can raise the specter of relativism. We think it is fair for students to ask, "If semiotics argues that values are culturally relative, then what's the point in having values?" Because such questions are difficult to answer, they sometimes are dismissed in a manner that suggests that some semioticians are eager to expose the ideological underpinnings of their opponents' values but that they consider their own values unassailable. We don't believe that this is a good way to teach semiotic thinking, so we'll address the issue of ethical relativism that semiotics raises in a more tentative way. We intend to open up the question for further debate—perhaps the first debate you may engage in with your class.

Our first response to the "What's the point, then?" question is that any attempt to devise an absolute standard of values is going to run into some trouble. Often, people rely on religious teachings to provide moral guidance, but it doesn't take long to see how ambiguous things can get even when we can agree on the same guide. American moral culture, for example, is founded on the injunctions of the Bible, whose commandment on killing seems clear enough. "Thou shalt not kill," the commandment says, but then the interpretation begins. Killing nonhumans is rarely included in the injunction (though in Buddhist culture, the ideal is to kill no animal at all), but what about war, capital punishment, euthanasia, and that most intractable of controversies, abortion? If your students begin to pronounce judgment on such matters, let the class discussion reveal the sources of their judgments. Likely as not there will be disagreement, and when students probe the ground for their opinions, they will discover that many such grounds are possible. Ask your class, then, who gets to decide which ground is paramount, and the ensuing discussion should reveal just how political our values are.

The point, then, is not whether value systems are possible, or which one is "obviously best"; it is how convincing we can be when presenting our values. Often, the challenge to justify one's opinions can illuminate their ideological foundations. Semiotic thinking teaches us to probe our values, not to give them up, and such probing can help us—especially as writers—find better ways of persuading others to adopt our point of view. Simply denouncing the opposition gets one nowhere: A writer has to find the terms that make the most sense to a reader who may not share his or her perspective. Indeed, as semioticians, we have written this text with the understanding that the semiotic point of view is hardly universal. But we firmly believe that, when thoughtfully presented, it can contribute to anyone's intellectual growth.

Using *Signs of Life in the U.S.A.*

Sample Syllabus

English Composition 3: Composition, Rhetoric, and Language

Spring 2015 Section 17 Tuesdays and Thursdays 12:30–1:45 Humanities A66

Sonia Maasik, Writing Programs Lecturer *Office: Humanities 140*
Phone: (310) 267-4680 *Mailbox: Humanities 146*
E-mail: maasik@humnet.ucla.edu *Office Hours: T, W, 10–12 & by appt.*

Course Description

English 3 is designed to develop students' critical reading and writing skills, including argumentation, analysis, style, grammar, and documentation conventions. Our section will focus on interpreting popular culture; because popular culture is part of our everyday lives, we often take for granted its profound effects on us. Thus, the course will also introduce a critical method called semiotics that

(Continued)

will enable you to go beyond the more obvious surface significance of a topic to a richer, more complex cultural analysis — the sort of analysis expected in university-level writing.

This course will be highly interactive: we'll have lots of whole-class discussion, of course, but also much small group work and student presentations. All this work is in the service of the course's ultimate goal: to strengthen your ability to write with power, impact, and confidence. To that end, we will also spend much time discussing writing strategies: developing persuasive arguments and insightful critical analysis; evaluating evidence; and devising an effective writing process that allows for strategic revision. By the end of the term, you will not only be more astute observers of the world around you; you'll also become a stronger writer ready to meet the challenges of academic work.

Textbooks (available at ASUCLA Bookstore)

Signs of Life in the U.S.A., 8th ed. (ed. Sonia Maasik and Jack Solomon) ISBN: 9781457670251 *A Writer's Reference*, 8th ed. (ed. Diana Hacker and Nancy Sommers) ISBN: 9781457666766

Course Requirements

- *Readings:* All materials should be read before the class for which they are assigned. Not doing the reading will produce unwanted pop quizzes; the grades for any such quizzes will affect your participation grade.
- *Reading/activity log:* Your log is meant to help you respond thoughtfully to your reading. For each day when a reading assignment is due, you need to bring to class a one- to two-page response (typed, double-spaced); in advance, I will give you questions to prompt your thinking. I will collect these responses on the day they are due, and I won't accept late responses. When evaluating your reading log, I will look for signs of thoughtful insights and careful responses to the issues you discuss. While your writing does not need to be stylistically formal, it should be grammatically correct and proofread for mechanical errors and typos. I will grade your logs on a check system. You are allowed to miss one response without penalty. **10% of course grade.**
- *Essays:* You'll write four formal essays, all of which require drafts that you will revise at home for final submission. On days that drafts are due, you need to bring three copies of complete drafts to class for peer review; this group activity will enable you to respond to others' work and to receive valuable feedback for revision. You are expected to make substantial revisions that transform the draft into a clearly written, thoughtfully argued essay. It is this revised draft that will receive a grade. You may also be asked to complete occasional short exercises, either in class or at home.

  It's important for you to keep up with your work. Late submission of work is not acceptable, but I grant you one "get-out-of-jail-free" card: you are allowed one late draft *or* revision without penalty. After you use your free pass, any late draft, revision, or Turnitin submission will result in 1/3 grade reduction for each day late (e.g., one day late means a B becomes a B– ; two days late means a B becomes a C+). If you submit a draft late, do not expect that your peers or I can respond to it. This class follows departmental policy that stipulates assignments more than one week late receive an F. **75% of course grade**.

- *Classwork/participation*: Your steady, active participation in discussions, small group work, peer review sessions, and presentations is essential to the success of this class. Please come to each class prepared to participate enthusiastically and thoughtfully. Because this work can't be "made up," tardiness, absences, and lack of participation will result in a lower course grade. **15% of course grade.**

Final Grade Breakdown

Essay #1 (4–5 pages): 15%
Essay #2 (5–6 pages): 20%
Essay #3 (5–6 pages): 20%
Essay #4 (7–8 pages): 30%
Reading log: 10%
Participation: 15%

Academic Honesty and Plagiarism

Presenting another author's words or ideas as your own, whether intentionally or not, is a serious offense, both in academia and in the professional world. The source can be verbal, textual, or electronic: taking material from a book or an article, your textbook, a class lecture or interview, the Internet, or any other source, and failing to attribute and document that source properly, constitutes plagiarism. Any paraphrase of another author's words or ideas also must be documented properly. UCLA takes plagiarism seriously: I am required to report any suspected case of plagiarism to the Office of the Dean of Students for investigation and possible disciplinary action. If you have any questions about when or how to document your sources, feel free to ask me at any time or consult *A Writer's Reference*. For further information about plagiarism and how to avoid it, consult the Dean of Students' Web site: http://www.deanofstudents.ucla.edu/Before%20You%Begin%That%20Paper.htm.

As a check on the proper use of sources, you will submit the final version of your essays to Turnitin (accessed through your course list on My.UCLA). You'll receive further instructions soon.

Tutoring Resources

The Undergraduate Writing Center (A61 Humanities, Powell Library 228, and 115 Rieber Hall) offers UCLA students one-on-one sessions that address individual writing issues. The Center is staffed by undergraduates trained to help at any stage in the writing process and with writing assignments from across the curriculum. Students can walk in, but appointments are preferred; online consultation is also available. For more information please call (310) 206-1320 or visit www.wp.ucla.edu and click on "Student Writing Center/Make an Appointment." Academic Advancement Program (AAP) students are encouraged to use AAP Tutorials (1114 Campbell Hall, 206-1581).

(Continued)

Students with Disabilities

If you wish to request an special arrangement due to a disability, please contact the Office for Students with Disabilities as soon as possible at A255 Murphy Hall, (310) 825-1501, (310) 206-6083 (telephone device for the deaf). Web site: www.osd.ucla.edu.

- *To pass the course, you must submit to me both a draft* ***and*** *a full revision for all three assignments.*
- *To satisfy UCLA's Writing I Requirement, you must earn a C or higher in English Comp. 3.*
- *Electronic devices must be turned off and stowed away during class time.*

Course Schedule

Each Thursday I'll post on our course Web site (www.ccle.ucla.edu) a more specific schedule that will include instruction on how to prepare for the following week's class sessions, prompts for your reading logs, due dates, and other crucial information. Readings from *A Writer's Reference* are identified as *WR*, followed by the section number to be read; all other readings are in *Signs of Life in the U.S.A.*

Unit One
Advertising and the Manufacturing of Our Identities

Week One
Tuesday:

- Course introduction; diagnostic writing exercise

Thursday:

- What is semiotics? How can it help us understand popular culture? *Read* "Popular Signs" and James A. Roberts, "The Treadmill of Consumption"
- Developing a strong thesis. *Read* "Writing About Popular Culture"; *WR* A1, A3–4

Week Two
Tuesday:

- How do advertisers use signs to encourage consumption? *Read* "Brought to You B(u)y: The Signs of Advertising"; James B. Twitchell, "What We Are to Advertisers"; and Joseph Turow, "The Daily You: How the New Advertising Industry Is Defining Your Identity and Your Worth"
- The writing process. *WR* C1–C3

Thursday:

- Advertising and the cult of cool. *Read* Thomas Frank, "Commodify Your Dissent" and Juliet B. Schor, "Selling to Children: The Marketing of Cool"

- Description vs. analysis and analyzing images. *Read* "Reading Visual Images Actively" and *WR* A2

Week Three
Tuesday:

- Advertising and the signs of class. *Read* Jack Solomon, "Masters of Desire: The Culture of American Advertising"
- Using sources properly. *Read* Scott Jaschik, "A Stand against Wikipedia"; Patti S. Caravello, "Judging Quality on the Web," and Trip Gabriel, "For Students in Internet Age, No Shame in Copy and Paste"
- Documentation conventions. *WR* MLA 1–4
- Draft thesis statement, essay #1, due (bring three copies of your thesis to class)

Thursday:

- Peer review session, essay #1 (bring three copies of your draft to class)

Week Four
Tuesday:

- Workshop: Revising your draft. *WR* G5, G6

Unit Two
Retail Culture, Signs, and the Construction of Consumer Behavior

Thursday:

- Analysis of retail space. *Read* Malcolm Gladwell, "The Science of Shopping" and Anne Norton, "The Signs of Shopping"

Week Five
Tuesday:

- The semiotics of packages. *Read* Thomas Hine, "What's in a Package"; bring to class a product package for discussion and analysis
- Organize teams for store project
- Due: Revision of assignment 1

Thursday:

- The meaning of possessions. *Read* Laurence Shames, "The More Factor" and Jon Mooallem, "The Self-Storage Self"; *WR* G1

Week Six
Tuesday:

- Group presentations: analysis of a store

(Continued)

Thursday:

- Strategies for revising prose: achieving directness, clarity; eliminating wordiness. *WR* W2, W5
- Draft of thesis statement, essay #2 due (bring three copies to class)

Week Six
Tuesday:

- Peer review session, assignment 2 (bring three copies of your draft to class)

Thursday:

- Workshop: Revising your draft. *WR* W3

Unit Three
The Cloud: Constructing Our Identities Online

Week Seven
Tuesday:

- Heads in The Cloud. *Read* "The Cloud: Semiotics and the New Media" and S. Craig Watkins, "Fast Entertainment and Multitasking in an Always-On World"

Thursday:

- The allure of social media. *Read* International Center for Media and the Public Agenda, "Students Addicted to Social Media" and Simon Dumenco, "If We're All So Sick of You, Facebook, Why Can't We Quit You?"

Week Eight
Tuesday:

- Defining ourselves in relation to our online lives. *Read* danah boyd, "Implications of User Choice: The Cultural Logic of 'MySpace or Facebook?'" and Rachel Lowry, "Straddling Online and Offline Profiles, Millennials Search for Identity"
- Due: Revision of assignment 2

Thursday:

- The ubiquity of technology. *Read* Salvador Rodriguez, "In the Digital Age, Breaking Up Is Hard to Do" and Stephanie Clifford and Quentin Hardy, "Attention, Shoppers: Store Is Tracking Your Cell"

Week Nine
Tuesday

- Culture in The Cloud. *Read* Henry Jenkins, "Convergence Culture"
- Draft of thesis statement, essay #3 due (bring three copies to class)

Thursday:

- Peer review session, essay #3 (bring three copies of your draft to class)

Unit Four
Nature, Culture, Consumerism: Constructing Our Identities

Week Ten
Tuesday:

- How do we develop our sense of identity? *Read* "My Selfie, My Self: Ma(s)king Identity in the New Millennium"
- Toys and the creation of young identities. *Read* Amy Lin, "Barbie: Queen of Dolls and Consumerism"

Thursday:

- The construction of gender identity. Read Aaron Devor, "Gender Role Behaviors and Attitudes"; Deborah Blum, "The Gender Blur: Where Does Biology End and Society Take Over?"; and Kevin Jennings, "American Dreams." *WR* W4

Week Eleven
Tuesday:

- Gender in the media. *Read* Steve Craig, "Men's Men and Women's Women," Jane Hu, "Reality Hunger: On Lena Dunham's *Girls*," Helena Andrews, "*The Butler* versus *The Help*: Gender Matters"

Thursday:

- Ethnicity and the creation of identity. *Read* Michael Omi, "In Living Color: Race and American Culture" and Jessica Hagedorn, "Asian Women in Film: No Joy, No Luck"

Week Twelve
Tuesday:

- Library orientation (meet in front of Powell Library at 12:25). *Read WR* R1–3

Thursday:

- How class may affect our sense of identity. *Read* Alfred Lubrano, "The Shock of Education: How College Corrupts," Michelle Dean, "Here Comes the Hillbilly, Again," and George Packer, "Celebrating Inequality"

Week Thirteen
Tuesday:

- Peer review session, essay #4 (bring three copies of your draft to class)

Thursday:

- Group conferences on revising your final essay

(Continued)

Week Fourteen
Tuesday:

- Brief presentations on revising final essay; revision workshop

Thursday:

- Class evaluations/course wrap-up

Finals Week
Monday

- Revision of assignment 4 due in my mailbox, Humanities 146, by 12:00 noon.

Sample Assignments

Assignment: Analysis of a Retail Space

Deadlines

Group Presentation: Wednesday, April 30
Draft Thesis Statement: Monday, May 5 (Bring three copies.)
Draft due: Wednesday, May 7 (Please bring three copies to class for peer review.)
Revision due: Monday, May 19 (Be sure to submit a hard copy of your revision, your peer review materials, and the draft that I read. Please submit your revision to Turnitin by 6:00 p.m.)

This assignment has two parts: (1) a small-group investigation of a store and a presentation to the class, and (2) an individually composed essay that analyzes the store.

(1) Group Work

- You will participate in some group work that should serve as a collective brainstorming session for your individual essay. In groups of five, you'll do an in-depth analysis of a store (we'll form groups and pick stores on April 23); on Wednesday, May 5, your group will give a 15-minute presentation that analyzes your retail outlet. All members of the group must participate in the presentation.
- On both April 25 and April 28, you'll have some time in class to meet with your group and plan your presentation. Before that, you should exchange e-mails and communicate outside class.

(2) Individual Essay Assignment
This assignment asks you to visit a retail store — it can be the one your group analyzes, or you can select another if you prefer. What you need to do is an inductive analysis that answers this question: **In what ways is the store designed to encourage consumption (if it is)? In other words, how does it use spatial signs to influence consumer behavior?** Some suggestions for approaching this task:

- "Inductive" means you start with details, then build to your thesis. So suspend your judgments as you start out and be a careful observer. Refer to the handout "Guidelines for Analyzing Retail Space" for suggestions about what to scrutinize.
- The primary question asked above does not assume that the store successfully stimulates consumption (or vice versa). Your judgment about that should inform your thesis, a statement that makes an overarching claim about how the store's design affects consumer behavior.
- You should use the Malcolm Gladwell essay as a critical framework for your analysis; the Anne Norton and Thomas Hine essays can also help you with your analysis. In addition, you may draw upon our discussions and readings about semiotics. But your focus should be on analyzing the store itself.

Length: 5–6 pages, double-spaced, one-inch margins all around, no larger than 12-point font, no extra space between paragraphs, please. Note: this is one inch: ______

Grading: This assignment is worth 25% of your final grade. Your contribution to the presentation will be included in the participation portion of your final grade.

Guidelines for Analyzing Retail Space

Use the following questions as a guide to your analysis of your chosen store. You don't need to consider all these questions—some may not even apply to your store—but they should help you to observe significant details.

1. The Store's Exterior
   - Are there window displays that feature merchandise? How are items arranged? How easily are they seen from the sidewalk? How simple are the displays?
   - What kind of signage identifies the store? To what extent does it attract customers?
   - Are there displays that extend out onto the sidewalk? What's their function? Are there decorative items (e.g., planters)?
   - To what extent is there a transitional zone from sidewalk to the entrance of the store?
   - What sort of establishments are located adjacent to this store? Are they ones that might inspire a pedestrian to walk more quickly?
2. The Store's Overall Layout and Design
   - Summarize the store's overall layout. What merchandise appears on the right and left of the entrance? The front and back of the store? Do you discern any logic to the arrangement of items?
   - Does the layout allow the customer to "downshift" upon entering the store?
   - What sort of merchandise or display appears at the store's entrance?

(Continued)

- How are aisles arranged? Where do they take you?
- Note the placement of tables, chairs, dressing rooms, restrooms. What logic underlies their placement?
- Note the relative location of featured/big ticket merchandise and small/impulse purchase items. Do you see any patterns?
- Note any in-store promotional displays. Where are they, and how obvious are they?
- Where is the check-out? How long are lines, and what are the consumers doing as they wait?
- To what extent do customers visit each section of the store?
- Can aisles accommodate strollers? Wheelchairs?
- Is music playing? What kind, and how does it contribute to the store's ambiance?

3. The Store's Customers

- Do you see any patterns in gender, age, ethnicity, appearance?
- Do customers tend to be alone or in groups? Does the store's design accommodate groups well?
- Where do consumers go first as they enter the store?
- Do customers look and leave, "grab and go" by product type, or browse? Does one type of shopping dominate?
- Do customers pay attention to in-store advertising? Which displays seem to capture their attention more?
- How long do customers stay in the store?
- Do customers handle/touch merchandise, or do they primarily just look at it?
- Do customers use the retail space in ways other than for which it is designed by developers?

Assignment: Analysis of a Children's Artifact

- *Rough draft due Wednesday, May 28 (bring three copies for peer review)*
- *Revision due Tuesday, June 10, by 12:00 noon in my box (146 Humanities). Please include the draft that I read and your peer review materials, and submit the revision to Turnitin by 6:00 p.m.*

This assignment asks you to conduct an in-depth analysis of a single product: a contemporary children's toy or game (that can include video games) that has human characteristics. Your overriding question should be in what ways does this toy socialize its young users to gender and/or racial norms? In order to construct your argument, draw upon class readings as well as the media/marketing context surrounding the object: the toy's packaging, marketing strategies (target age group, placement in stores, print advertisements, television commercials), merchandising (clothing, décor, and accessories), Web sites (home pages, shops), related media (cartoons, movies, video games, books), and consumer feedback (reviews on Web sites, interviews with children and/or parents). I don't expect you to consider all these possibilities; they are just that, possibilities. But I do expect you to go beyond the toy itself to consider the larger system through which the toy constructs gender/racial codes.

Many of our course readings — on advertising, store design, packaging, gender, and ethnicity — can help give you a critical framework for your analysis, and I invite you to use them. But I want you to develop your own analysis. This is *not* an assignment that asks you to review the research literature on your topic, so I do *not* want you to rely on essays that present so-and-so's research on how children's notions of gender roles are affected by X category of toy. I want you to study the toy and its media context and draw your own conclusions. And when you study that media context, don't take it at face value: you need to analyze it, not use promotional claims as your own.

Length: 6 pages with standard one-inch margins, 12-point font. Please include any print ads or copies of Internet ads and the like. This essay is worth 30% of your final grade.

Note: For the last assignment, you cannot use your "get-out-of-jail-free" card for the revision.

Assignment: Researched Semiotic Analysis

Your assignment is to choose **one** (1) of the following television topics: *Girls, Sons of Anarchy*, or *The Simpsons*, and write a complete cultural-semiotic analysis of it using the techniques that we have studied this semester. To perform your analysis **you must construct a *system* of *associated* and *differentiated* popular cultural phenomena in which to situate and interpret your topic**, and you must research the relevant *history* of your topic in order to construct the system in which it fits. To do this you will need to identify the *genre* of television show your topic belongs to and include this as part of your analysis. You must also consider the cultural *codes* involved in your topic (including relevant *gender codes, racial overtones,* and/or *cultural mythologies*, as well as any relevant *cultural contradictions*). Do not simply write a report, a plot summary alone, or puff piece: your paper must be a semiotic analysis with an interpretive argument pertaining to what you think the topic you choose *signifies about American culture and consciousness*.

Your analysis must consider the TV program you choose both as a whole (that is, its overall theme or concept) and with respect to an individual episode. Guidance on how to analyze television concepts and episodes can be found in *Signs of Life in the U.S.A.* 8th edition on pages 28–30; 41–49; and 259–62. Consider also the **advertising** that accompanies the show for clues about its intended audience.

To conduct your analysis you will have to research your topic and its related cultural signifiers in the system that you construct. Your research must include both print and electronic sources (television and movies or DVDs, along with

(Continued)

YouTube videos and TV advertisements, count as electronic sources, as does the Internet; the readings in *Signs of Life* can also be used as print sources, but they must be properly documented). You must have at least **seven** (7) sources for your paper. Instructions on how to document your sources can be found on pages 66–69 in *Signs of Life in the U.S.A.* If you have any questions concerning documentation, please ask the instructor of the class.

Your paper must be given a title that not only identifies your topic but also suggests what you are going to say about it (e.g., "The Racial Significance of Skinny Jeans").

Your papers must be **in the close range of 3000 words** (typed double-spaced according to MLA documentation standards).

You are responsible for following all of the instructions on this assignment sheet.

Alternative Thematic Arrangements

You're not likely to march through *Signs of Life* chapter by chapter, assigning your students every selection; even if you want to do that, you probably won't have time. You'll probably use the text selectively to accommodate the length of your school term and the skill level of your students. There are better and worse ways to do that. One way, of course, is to cover the entire text but eliminate readings from each chapter. We advise against this simply because your students may feel frustrated by what can seem a whirlwind tour of topics (the "if it's Tuesday, it must be film" feeling). We've deliberately designed the book to create a cross-pollination of topics throughout the text. Our culture's assumptions about race, for instance, shape how ethnicity is represented in film, which in turn may perpetuate or undermine those assumptions; similarly, prevailing beliefs about gender are reinforced and legitimized through advertising, TV, and film.

So what do we recommend? We suggest that you begin with the general Introduction so that students can gain an overview of the book, understand the semiotic approach, and learn why they're covering popular culture in their writing class. At this point, you might ask them for their ideas on which selections they'd like to cover. Although it may seem scary to begin the course without everything mapped out in detail, you may win greater class involvement if you allow your students some say in what they have to read. As an alternative, you could plan out the first half of the course, then solicit student suggestions for the second half. If you prefer more structure, we see two possible approaches: (1) organizing your course around one broad theme or (2) creating several small units, each with its own theme.

Organizing your course around one broad theme. Three of the chapters — "Consuming Passions: The Culture of American Consumption" (Chapter 1), "Heroes and Villains: Encoding Our Conflicts" (Chapter 6), and "My Selfie, My Self: Ma(s)king Identity in the New Millennium" (Chapter 7) — address themes far-ranging enough that focus your entire course on one. After beginning with one of these chapters and covering it entirely, you could pick among other chapters that contain readings related to the theme and select readings that would best enhance your approach to the overall topic. The following possibilities would work well for these three broad topics.

Theme: Consuming Behavior in America
Begin with "Consuming Passions" (Chapter 1).
Assign "Brought to You B(u)y" (Chapter 2).

Pick from the following: Nick Serpe, "Reality Pawns: The New Money TV" (Chapter 3); S. Craig Watkins, "Fast Entertainment and Multitasking in an Always-On World" (Chapter 5); George Packer, "Celebrating Inequality" (Chapter 6); Rachel Lowry, "Straddling Online and Offline Profiles, Millennials Search for Identity" (Chapter 7).

Theme: Heroes and Villains
Begin with "Heroes and Villains: Encoding Our Conflicts" (Chapter 6).
Pick from the following: Thomas Frank, "Commodify Your Dissent" (Chapter 1); Jack Solomon, "Masters of Desire: The Culture of American Advertising" (Chapter 2); "Video Dreams: Television and Cultural Forms" (Chapter 3); "The Hollywood Sign: The Culture of American Film" (Chapter 4); Theresa Celebran Jones, "*Sanjay and Craig:* Nickelodeon's Hilarious New Mixed-Race Heroes" (Chapter 7).

Theme: Identity
Begin with "My Selfie, My Self: Ma(s)king Identity in the New Millennium" (Chapter 7).
Pick from the following: Jon Mooallem, "The Self-Storage Self" (Chapter 1); Jack Solomon, "Masters of Desire: The Culture of American Advertising" (Chapter 2); James B. Twitchell, "What We Are to Advertisers" (Chapter 2); Joseph Turow, "The Daily You" (Chapter 2); Jane Hu, "Reality Hunger: On Lena Dunham's *Girls*" (Chapter 3); David Denby, "High-School Confidential: Notes on Teen Movies" (Chapter 4); S. Craig Watkins, "Fast Entertainment and Multitasking in an Always-On World" (Chapter 5); International Center for Media & the Public Agenda, "Students Addicted to Social Media" (Chapter 5); danah boyd, "Implications of User Choice: The Cultural Logic of 'MySpace or Facebook?'" (Chapter 5).

Creating several small units, each with its own theme. Because the selections cover many interrelated themes, you could organize your course around several focused topics. You'll probably spot such units as you skim through the book; we suggest some here that we find especially appealing. By no means is this a definitive list, nor should you feel obligated to cover all the readings suggested for each theme.

Ethnicity/Multiculturalism
Assign Michael Omi, "In Living Color" (Chapter 7).
Pick from the following: Stanford, Dean, Paskin (Chapter 3); Hagedorn, Andrews, Seitz, Folch (Chapter 4); Packer, Wilke (Chapter 6); McClain, Jones, Christian (Chapter 7).

Gender
Assign Aaron Devor, "Gender Role Behaviors and Attitudes" and Deborah Blum, "The Gender Blur: Where Does Biology End and Society Take Over?" (Chapter 7).
Pick from the following: Norton (Chapter 1); Craig, Pozner, Steinem (Chapter 2); Stanford, Dean, Simons, Hu, Paskin (Chapter 3); Hagedorn, Andrews, Denby (Chapter 4); Rodriguez (Chapter 5); Jennings, Nelson, McClain (Chapter 7).

Interpreting Signs and Images
Assign "Popular Signs: Or, Everything You've Always Known About American Culture (But Nobody Asked)"; "Writing about Popular Culture"; frontispieces, images, and photos throughout the text.

Pick from the following: Gladwell, Norton, Hine, Mooallem, Japp and Japp, Frank (Chapter 1); Solomon, Craig, Pozner, Schor, Corbett, Portfolio of Ads (Chapter 2); Serpe, Stanford, Dean, Simons, Gabler (Chapter 3); Hagedorn, Denby, Parenti, Agresta, Folch (Chapter 4); Watkins, boyd (Chapter 5); Gittell, Wilke (Chapter 6); Devor, Jennings, Nelson, Omi, Christian (Chapter 7).

Social Class

Pick from the following: Shames, Mooallem (Chapter 1); Twitchell, Turow (Chapter 2); Serpe, Dean, Hu, Paskin (Chapter 3); Andrews, Parenti (Chapter 4); boyd (Chapter 5), Packer, Gittell (Chapter 6); Jennings, Lubrano (Chapter 7).

Personal Privacy and Threats to It

Pick from the following: Gladwell, Clifford and Hardy, Roberts (Chapter 1); Twitchell, Steinem, Turow (Chapter 2); International Center for Media & the Public Agenda, Rodriguez, Rushfield, D'Addario (Chapter 5); Lowry (Chapter 7).

Encouraging Student Response and Involvement

Signs of Life presumes a class with active students, calling upon their knowledge of popular culture and encouraging them to be lively participants in class. We've built into the apparatus suggestions for a variety of ways students can respond to readings, reflect on them, and discuss them with others. We've tried to suggest responses that are appropriate to each reading. For instance, we include at least one reflective journal topic for selections that might disturb readers. But we intend our suggestions to be flexible: Just because we frame a topic as an essay question, for instance, doesn't mean that you can't rewrite it as a journal prompt. We'll summarize for you the major strategies we've relied on to trigger student response, and we'll offer whatever hints we can for ensuring their success.

Introduction We consider the general Introduction essential if you plan to use the semiotic approach, for that's where we not only explain the method and our rationale for using it but also walk students through sample interpretations that can serve as models for their own analyses. Notice that often we stop short of completing an analysis. We've deliberately not provided definitive readings of the topics raised; instead, we try to give just enough so that students will be excited and encouraged to move beyond what we say to pursue their own interpretations. In class, ask your students to finish the job, to amplify and extend, or even to contradict the analyses that we've started. Even if you don't use semiotics, the Introduction explains why this textbook focuses on popular culture as its topic.

Writing about Popular Culture We recognize that many students, even early in their writing process, may want to see what a "real" essay looks like as a model to guide their own revision and thinking. We've thus included in our Introduction suggestions for writing on popular culture, and because many instructors ask their students to analyze visual texts, we include a section offering advice on how to do that. We also include student-written essays on topics prompted by this text. Of course, you may wish to supplement this material with sample essays written by your own students. But these sample essays are particularly useful if you want to review student work early in the term before your own students have produced final drafts, or you may prefer the diplomatically easier choice of critiquing an essay not written by someone sitting in class.

This section has two parts: an introduction to writing about popular culture and three sample student essays. You can assign the introductory comments with or without the subsequent essays — the two can exist independently. The introductory material is best assigned early in the term, perhaps even before students start their first writing assignment. Here we emphasize prewriting strategies, especially critical reading strategies and invention techniques, and offer suggestions on writing arguments about popular culture. Specifically, we emphasize constructing a strong argument with specific evidence — one of the most common needs of students, even at varying levels and abilities, is to learn how to translate their personal reactions and private opinions into a defensible argument that can stand up in the court of public discussion. Then we walk students through the beginnings of an interpretation of an ad to demonstrate some of the strategies they can use when they need to analyze a visual text. Our comments are intended not to be exhaustive, but rather to suggest to your students how academic discourse demands that writers be responsible to their readership in addition to their own ideas.

The second part presents three student essays, chosen because they represent a range of styles and topics, with brief marginal annotations. While we believe each writer is effective in achieving his or her goals, be aware that, as with any student writing, there's always room for improvement. So we suggest you describe these essays not as "ideal" models — that might intimidate some students — but as interesting and effective responses to some of the issues *Signs of Life* raises. If your students can suggest revisions to strengthen the essays, great!

The first essay, by Amy Lin of UCLA, presents a full-dress analysis of Barbie that focuses less on gender issues than on the way the doll — and the marketing system to which it belongs — promotes consumerism. Here you'll want to note the array of sources the student uses, from Internet to journal articles, and her superb handling of specific detail. (We also like her sense of humor and personal voice.) We include the second essay, by Rose Sorooshian of California State University, Northridge, because it's an excellent example of a full-blown semiotic analysis of *The Walking Dead* (and other zombie-focused hits), analyzing the program's popularity through the economic and social context in which it thrived. The third student essay, by Ryan Kim of UCLA, is a tidy analysis of *Gran Torino*; we include it because he does a particularly nice job of dissecting the often contradictory racial signs in this film.

Advice on Selecting and Citing Sources As researchers and teachers, we know what a boon the Internet has been in conducting research, learning about new topics, and finding excellent source material; our students, however, typically are not so savvy in evaluating the appropriateness and credibility of online sources. Often they cannot discern the difference between a reputable source and a commercial site, and frequently they mistake advocacy sites for sources of factual information. And all too commonly, they rely upon a source such as Wikipedia, without realizing that an encyclopedia-style source is not appropriate for a college essay and that the materials on Wikipedia are not vetted. Indeed, we've seen that many a student has adopted the habit of, shall we say, "extending" an essay through extensive quotation from Wikipedia, providing information that simply does not need to be in an essay. (We recall, for instance, nearly a full page defining what a pickup truck is, courtesy of Wikipedia — we kid you not.) Thus, we include three articles that should help guide your students in selecting appropriate sources: Scott Jaschik's "A Stand against Wikipedia," Patti S. Caravello's "Judging Quality on the Web," and Trip Gabriel's "For Students in the Internet Age, No Shame in Copy and Paste."

As in the previous editions, we also include a brief guide to citing sources, including online and media sources, for your students' quick reference.

Frontispieces and Images We feel that it's essential for a semiotics-based reader to include both images and text, so each chapter begins with a frontispiece that presents an image related to the chapter's topic, and throughout the book appear photos and images ripe for analysis. Discuss these images with your students, perhaps as a way to begin class discussion of a new topic. What are both the immediate impact the images have on them — their gut responses — and the images' cultural and social significance? To get your students thinking about an issue, ask them to brainstorm alternative images and then to debate which ones they would or would not want to see in a text. Not only would such a discussion reveal much about their own worldviews, it would enable students to see that they've already been semioticians all along.

Chapter Introductions and Boxed Questions A crucial part of the book, the chapter introductions suggest ways to analyze the chapter's subject and provide a critical framework for reading and understanding the essays that follow. Such a framework is vital for a popular-culture textbook, for the students' strengths can become their weaknesses. Because students know so much about the culture around them, it's sometimes hard for them to adopt a critical stance toward it; guiding students toward that critical stance is one of the introductions' main tasks. The introductions suggest ways to read a subject, model interpretations of examples, link the various issues raised by the selections, and (as with the general Introduction) create opportunities for students to explore a question further. You can also trigger discussion by assigning the boxed questions included with each introduction. The "Exploring the Signs" questions are all journal or prewriting topics, intended to stimulate a student's thinking on a topic even before you discuss it in class. Most relate a chapter's subject to the student's personal experience, and they're meant to help students connect a broad or abstract topic to their own lives. The "Discussing the Signs" boxes suggest in-class activities such as debates, discussions, or small-group work. You could try these tasks either on the day you discuss the chapter introduction or anytime when you're covering the chapter readings. The "Reading on the Net" exercises suggest ways to investigate a topic on the Internet. Some Net exercises send students online to research a topic; others ask them to interpret what they find on a given Web site. You can also have your students research the background behind pop culture phenomena, an especially useful strategy if you want them to have some historical range in their analyses. In some cases, we've given specific Internet addresses, but recall that the Net is always changing — your students may find alternative sites that are as interesting as the ones we've suggested.

"Reading the Text" Questions All selections are accompanied first by questions we've dubbed "Reading the Text," essentially comprehension questions designed to ensure careful, accurate reading. They ask students to identify the selections' key concepts, explain difficult terms, and articulate how the selections' main ideas relate to each other and to the evidence the authors present. These questions are ideal for readings logs or journals. You could routinely assign them whenever you give a reading assignment, or you could assign them just for selections you expect may be difficult for your students. We suggest creating some mechanism whereby your students can share their responses with others. You might begin discussion of a reading by asking some students to read their responses to the class; that will enable you to see quickly whether your students had any trouble understanding the selection. Alternatively, your students could share their responses in small groups, or they might write brief responses on the board at the beginning of class.

"Reading the Signs" Questions Each selection is also accompanied by various writing and activity questions designed to produce clear analytic thinking and strong student writing. You'll see that most "Reading the Signs" questions call for a written response to the text. Some we've framed as journal topics; we find it pedagogically valuable for students to be able to link sometimes abstract or theoretical concepts to their own lives. Seeing that their schoolwork doesn't have to exist independently of their home culture can prove a tremendous motivation for students. Journal entries can also be particularly useful for selections that might disturb your students, as they can allow them a chance to explore their responses before they get to class. Occasionally, you might ask students to read their entries aloud in small groups or before the entire class (for sensitive topics, you might read the entries to the class yourself, without revealing the students' names). But be sure to let your class know at the beginning of the term whether the journal will be public (shared with other students) or private (shared with just you), or both.

The essay questions range from fairly simple and straightforward to challenging and controversial, calling for different modes of response (argumentation, comparison, and so forth). Some topics focus on a single selection, whereas others ask students to consider two or more selections in relation to each other. You'll find that some questions ask students to conduct research, both traditional and nontraditional, such as interviews. We've found that students become excited when doing such work and that they often produce their best writing when they can generate their own primary evidence. To ensure successful interviews, you should provide them with some guidelines ahead of time. First, let them understand that an inductive research process may feel messier than a deductive one: That's not a problem as long as they realize how their writing process may differ. In addition, discuss with your students some key interviewing strategies, such as the difference between open-ended questions and those that prompt yes–no responses, and ask them to prepare interview questions for your review. Your students can benefit from role-playing, conducting short interviews in class. Role-playing can help them with timing; students usually underestimate how long it will take to cover a set of questions.

A number of prompts invite other in-class activities such as group work, debates, and hypothetical conversations. We encourage you to try these to stimulate all your students to participate. We've found small groups can work for almost any sort of class activity, from discussing a selection to writing a collaborative research paper. Small groups often allow students to be more honest, and being in a group can make it easier for quiet students to participate. We particularly like that groups can change up the class dynamics. In addressing gender issues, for instance, you can create same-sex groups to discuss a topic and then have the groups report to the whole class. That way not only will students benefit from their group discussion, but they can stand back and examine the groups themselves for evidence of gender-based patterns. One kind of group work that can yield surprising results is a hypothetical conversation between two authors or characters from the readings. We like these conversations because students must first discuss among themselves the likely positions each author would take on a topic (*what* the author would say); then they must consider the manner of presentation appropriate for each author (*how* the author would say it). If you ask your students to stage such a conversation, be sure to give them enough time to plan it — that's when much of the learning takes place!

Debates are particularly valuable for teaching argumentative strategies: Students must generate logical arguments, amass compelling evidence, and anticipate opposing viewpoints. When creating debate teams, we've found it works best to mix students of various viewpoints — in other words, it's not necessary for everyone on a team to hold the same opinion about an issue. If the group members have different opinions, they will be exposed to alternative positions when planning their presentations. We should add that our goal behind staging student debates is to encourage them to see alternatives and acknowledge the shades of gray that muddle any substantive intellectual question (not to lead students to pro/con thinking).

Some questions call for nonanalytic assignments, such as designing an advertisement. Give these a try; they provide students a chance to put the analytical and theoretical material to practical use. Students may see such assignments as just fun, so we suggest that you create some mechanism whereby they reflect on or analyze their creations. They might present their work to the class, explaining the rationale behind it, or, in an essay, they could describe their goals and discuss the extent to which their creation fulfilled those goals.

Glossary of Key Terms We include a glossary of key words and concepts drawn from the chapter introductions to provide a ready reference for you and your students.

***LaunchPad Solo for* Signs of Life in the U.S.A.** Promote digital literacy and practice rhetorical skills with LaunchPad Solo, an assignable and customizable digital learning platform that includes interactive tutorials on critical reading and working with sources, LearningCurve adaptive quizzing, and e-readings that encourage students to think critically about multimodal and online texts, including vintage ads, film clips, and other artifacts of popular culture — all designed to work in tandem with your textbook. These sources are available for free when packaged with the textbook; you can find more information at **macmillanhighered.com/signsoflife.**

Signs of Life Blog Free of charge, the blog is located at http://blogs.bedfordstmartins.com/bits/author/solomon/ and includes postings on teaching pop culture in the composition classroom as well as semiotic interpretations of topics drawn from recent events and entertainments. This is a good place to find semiotic takes on movies and other pop culture phenomena that will inevitably occur after the publication of this textbook and can help stimulate class discussion on up-to-the-minute topics. Written by Jack Solomon on a bi-weekly basis during the academic year, the blog has discussed such topics as *Game of Thrones* and *Girls*, the value of the Humanities and the politics of MOOCs (massive open online courses), and the cultural politics of movies like *Thor* and *Frozen*. Instructors and students alike are encouraged to respond with comments of their own on this interactive site.

Advice from Experienced Instructors

Since we began working on the first edition of *Signs of Life* over twenty years ago, we have benefited from the fresh ideas and innovative teaching techniques of our friends and colleagues — and we'd like to share some of this helpful advice with you. Meredith Kurz of Valley College in Van Nuys, California, provides suggestions for an array of pedagogical issues ranging from sequencing assignments throughout the term to preventing plagiarism. Next, Deborah Banner describes an imaginative class project that she assigned at UCLA, involving group work, student presentations, the collaborative creation of an ad, and individual student essays. We find their ideas striking and believe you will as well, whether you're new to *Signs of Life* or a veteran.

MEREDITH KURZ

Signs of Life in the Composition Class

My title's obviously pilfered wordplay echoes what I believe to be the spirit of this textbook and its perhaps secondary or tertiary message — that a somewhat less than deadly serious approach to the subject of composition and composition pedagogy is not undesirable. When all is said and done, to write is to play, and to teach writing also is to play — to play with ideas, writing techniques, grammar, and words. The problem I faced in teaching my early semesters was that I had not yet found my own way to that realization; consequently, there was no way that I could help my students find their own way there. But because lately I have made some modest progress in that respect, I submit my roadmap for perusal by both novice and seasoned instructors. It is marked with concepts, directions, tips, and other miscellanea that I have picked up along the way from professorial mentors, collegial colleagues, and anyone else who had something to offer and did.

During the first of my university's two teaching assistant training semesters, my composition director gave our class some very useful advice: "Get a good textbook, and let it support you," she said. With this idea in mind, we TAs set about finding the most supportive book available and chose for our first-teaching-semester textbook a reader-rhetoric-handbook combination. We were motivated to select such a text for three reasons:

- For our students' sakes (having everything included in one book would lower course costs for them);
- Because of our own insecurities (this textbook was so complete that it could teach the course all by itself; then we would be able to relax and cruise right through our first semester because "we had a good textbook, and we were going to let it support us"); and
- Because our instructor advised us to choose that particular textbook.

That first semester, I cleaved to that book with religious fervor, presenting the text to my students, chapter and verse, rigidly following the order of the textbook from Chapter 1 forward. Then, somewhere around mid-semester, I realized that I was losing my class's interest and my own energy. My undeviating progress through the textbook was boring me to death, and I seemed to be taking my students with me. Certainly, none of us were turning out any deathless prose. This complete textbook dependence on my part fostered a rigidity that worked to stifle almost all the original ideas anyone might have had, to abort any innovative writing styles that may have been gestating in my students' minds, and to suffocate whatever creative teaching I might have attempted.

Fortunately, at about that time, my composition director gave our TA class (many of whom found themselves in a similar situation) a second very useful bit of advice: "Don't allow your textbook to control you," she said. At first, this new useful advice seemed to contradict the old useful advice, until I realized that support and control are two entirely different concepts. At that point, I decided to change to a less prescriptive textbook format so that I wouldn't be tempted to lean so heavily on it. Accordingly, I set about finding a book that would afford my students and me a greater degree of flexibility, offer some not unwanted guidance, and yet not encourage dependence. Please forgive me if I sound like a textbook commercial here, but it was just about then that *Signs of Life in the U.S.A.* (hereinafter affectionately referred to as *SOL*) came into my life—just in time to breathe some life into my teaching. A reader with something extra, *SOL* provided both the readings and the "way" for my class and for me. *SOL* is a textbook that offers instructive, but not pedantic, readings and that provides a flexible and dynamic analytical methodology for reading and for writing. Additionally, the sheer number and diversity of essays make the textbook adaptable to many different types of semester formats, allowing room for instructor creativity and providing enough material for a multitude of assignment focuses.

I also welcomed the move from division by modes—to my mind, a rather outmoded and useless structure—to this text's focus on popular culture, semiotic methodology, and subject-oriented organization. The textbook's content, approach, and arrangement are such that anyone from anywhere can find material of interest and a way to write about it. Equally important, however, I also found in *SOL* room to play and flexible rules to play by. Although it may have been too late to resurrect my first semester, I had found a way to infuse life into my second.

Here ends the testimonial for *SOL* and begins some (I hope) useful suggestions for its application.

My Choice: The Assignment-Driven Semester

Some colleges and universities supply to their composition faculty a departmentally mandated textbook and require that the composition course follow its usually prescriptive text. I have been fortunate enough never to have worked in such circumstances except in my first TA semester. The English departments for which I have taught generally have given me a wide choice of textbooks as well as the discretion to formulate my semester as I see fit. Each has supplied me with only a very general course outline that allows for a great deal of creativity on my part. These course outlines vary little from school to school and seem to adhere to the following broad assignment pattern: (1) the narrative essay, (2) the analysis essay, (3) the argument essay, and (4) the research essay. Making semester planning a bit more complex, at California State University, Northridge, where I did my TA training and teaching, the department required, in addition to the class textbook, a full-text nonfiction work as well.

My first semester's semi-disaster served me when I devised my second assignment. I learned a lot from that experience, and one important lesson involved that first essay assignment — the narrative. In that first semester, most students turned in narratives that were exclusive rather than inclusive. These essays could not have been of interest to anyone but the writer herself and maybe, just maybe, her best friend. The writing was far too personal and, unfortunately, set a tone for the semester that I found difficult to dislodge. Subsequent essays, no matter what their purpose, always seemed to emerge from a too-personal point of view and consequently spoke only to an exclusive audience, no matter what purpose and audience directives I had supplied. I realized that the problem had a great deal to do with the students' rhetorical maturity and that it was my job to move them from their writing adolescence into a writing adulthood. Clearly, I needed to set up a model that would move them from "I" to "we" and finally to "they" — from subjective to intersubjective, to objective, the academic objective being the writing style that they needed to acquire. My goal would be to achieve a synthesis between the four types of essays required and the three rhetorical stances I wished to move them through.

My Unit I: Narrative (The Inclusive "I")

My whole text, Mike Rose's excellent autobiographical narrative *Lives on the Boundary* (New York: Penguin, 1990) provided a perfect jumping off point for the semester. Rose writes an autobiographical narrative that is "I" oriented but also discusses many other issues, literacy among them, and literacy, after all, is what we are after in our classes. After two weeks spent reading, discussing, and writing about the Rose narrative, it was an easy segue into *SOL*, where I began by assigning a personal literacy narrative. The assignment asked them to write either a cultural autobiography, a cultural biography, or a literacy narrative and, like the authors of their textbook models, to write inclusively rather than exclusively.

My Unit II: Analysis (The Cultural "We")

In the second unit, students moved from a subjective to an intersubjective point of view, focusing on how we construct and know ourselves as individuals within our own cultures and how we relate as members of or visitors to American culture, in particular. We all need to understand the worldview within which we must operate. To begin,

I assigned the general Introduction to *SOL* so that students could apprehend the central focus and critical methodology that would support their reading and writing in Units II, III, and IV of the course. At this point, I began really to "let my textbook support me." I made good use of the boxed questions embedded in the text of the Introduction for freewriting and journal writing. I also encouraged students to question the text itself and then attempt to answer their own questions either in group discussions or in individual journal entries. Because the Introduction informs the reader of the constructed mythological underpinnings of all they know and believe, I consider it fitting that students question any possible mythological bases for the textbook authors' stance as well. I want them to question everything!

Next, we read the introductions to Chapter 1, "Consuming Passions: The Culture of American Consumption," and Chapter 2, "Brought to You B(u)y: The Signs of Advertising," along with selected essays from each of these chapters, to learn how "we" come to be products of our shared cultures. I found Laurence Shames's "The More Factor" (Chapter 1) to be a real eye-opener to the basic American myth and its all-pervasive influence on our national psyche. I then moved from the general principles of the myth to some of the manifestations. Finally, selections such as Jack Solomon's "Masters of Desire: The Culture of American Advertising" (Chapter 2) helped all of us to understand some of the ways in which we disseminate and perpetuate that myth.

Working through these first two chapters prepared the students to write their second essay of the semester, an analysis for which I gave them a rather broad directive: They could analyze a trend, a style, a fad, or an advertisement. Then, with Units I and II under our belts, we were ready to go on to my Units III and IV.

My Unit III: Argument (The Position Paper)

About halfway through the semester, we made the giant leap from subjective to objective writing, understanding that writing, either from "I" or "we," never allows us to be wholly objective. We now focused our discussions and writing exercises outside of ourselves as we examined some of the issues featured in the textbook as well as some too new to have made it into the latest edition. Once we had worked through one issue chapter, reading the introduction and then at least three or four essays, the students acquired a basic understanding of how to address an issue. The textbook essays modeled for them how to examine an issue by presenting and interpreting data and then taking a position and supporting it. Chapter 7, "My Selfie, My Self: Ma(s)king Identity in the New Millennium" (as well as readings on race, class, and gender woven throughout the other chapters) generally is of interest to students because the readings deal with concerns that touch or have touched their lives. The readings in these chapters stimulated very active classroom discussion and some intense freewriting and journaling. Since students had by now liberated their writing from self, it seemed appropriate that their third essay assignment allow them a greater degree of latitude. Accordingly, for this assignment, they had the freedom to interact with any essay or essays from either one of the issue chapters we'd covered or to select an essay from one of the other issue chapters.

In addition, while we were working in this unit, students had the opportunity to begin integrating information from source texts into their writing (a skill that they would need to develop for their fourth major essay assignment). Furthermore, by interacting with one or more of the textbook essays, they learned not only to interact with other writers (by including a voice or voices other than their own in their writing) but also to work with the conventions of integrating and citing sources according to MLA guidelines. After that, it was onward to the final assignment of the semester.

My Unit IV: Research (The Academic Objective)

Now that my students had experienced taking a supported position using textual evidence in the argument essay, they were ready for the final challenge of the semester, the research paper. I never have been in favor of pointless research essays that are nothing more than information dumps; therefore, I required that the research essay make some kind of point and express a thesis, whether stated or implied. At this point, I made good use of *SOL*'s model student essays located in "Writing about Popular Culture." The students had already read this section before writing their first essay, but I encouraged them to reread it each time they began a new assignment.

For this assignment, even more than the previous one, I also relied on the textbook to supply the subject bases for the students' papers and to act as the primary research resource as well. I did this with good reason.

Reason 1: To Plagiarism-Proof the Paper (well, almost)

Unfortunately, the plagiarism problem continues to exist, exacerbated by one of our best new research tools, the Internet. Not only do students turn in papers borrowed from friends or culled from sorority or fraternity files, but they also download papers from cyberfiles full of essays for sale. One way of circumventing the problem is to construct a research essay assignment that, like the argument paper, bounces off a textbook essay, thereby helping to ensure that students will not be able to submit a borrowed or purchased paper. I find that requiring my students to integrate two *SOL* essays in with their other sources to create the finished product allows little opportunity for plagiarism. This is another example of how allowing my textbook to support me helps me to maintain control in a critical area.

Reason 2: Creating Interesting Concept Connections and Facilitating Research

One thought-provoking way to construct the research assignment is to have the students not only address the issue itself but also examine the ways that media present it. Taking this approach, students can make use of both the textbook issue section they've chosen and one or more of the media-focused chapters. With the textbook as their primary research resource, they have access to a number of essays from which to draw, and of course they can and must move outside of it to find additional material in the university's library and on the Internet. (I do limit the number of allowable Internet sources to two.) Using the textbook in this way, my students have turned out some extremely successful research papers.

I have continued to use *SOL* in subsequent semesters, always finding new ways to use its content and method. It's just like the mythical magic purse: Each time I spend some of it, the expenditure increases rather than decreases its content for me.

Still More Support

Throughout the semester, the students can enhance their active, critical reading skills by using the questions headed "Reading the Text" for reading journal entries. These questions encourage students not simply to read but to interact critically with the text to formulate their answers. I save the questions listed under the "Reading the Signs" heading for in-class work: freewriting, group discussions, group exercises, and other productive activities I otherwise would have to invent. These questions engage students in evaluating and analyzing the material content of the essay and their own points of view in relation to the material.

Here, again, I allow the textbook to support me. It is awfully hard work to come up with interesting writing prompts, whether for journal entries, freewrites, group activities, or formal essay assignments. Instructors spend many hours devising these kinds of questions, as did I during my first TA semester. It's a wonderful relief to let the textbook do more of that work so that I have the time, energy, and freedom to enjoy my job and to teach my students that writing need not be drudgery, but an interesting, involving, and immensely enjoyable and rewarding pastime.

Finally, I want to reemphasize the point that accepting this kind of support does not amount to allowing the textbook to control my semester or me. I still make all the major decisions. I construct my semester, select the essays I want my students to read, make the assignments, and decide exactly how semiotic I want us to be. The choices are all mine. *SOL* allows me that degree of latitude. And what of the rhetorical art—invention, form, and style? In my experience so far, students learn more from reading good, interesting writing and then writing, writing, writing, themselves than they ever will learn from reading the dry passages found in many rhetorics and handbooks. What extra information I think they need concerning invention, form, and style I can supply from my own education and experience as a college reader and writer. We all can. We've made it this far: We must know something!

DEBORAH BANNER

Undergraduates in Grey Flannel Suits: Advertising in the Composition Classroom

On one unusually crisp Monday afternoon in November, a corporate behemoth took over my English composition classroom. Five creative teams vied for financial and administrative support as they presented advertising strategies for new consumer products to their supervisors. Each team unveiled a new product, discussed marketing plans, and debuted original print and video ads. Unlike most marketing meetings, however, this one ended in an awards ceremony at which each group received certificates of achievement and rousing ovations. Also unlike most meetings, every participant submitted a five-page paper to the "Executive Vice President"—actually, me—at the end of the session.

It sounds elaborate, but to my students, that Monday was just another deadline for their fall class in composition, rhetoric, and language. They were used to odd pedagogical shenanigans—I had already impersonated a talk-show host, a fitness instructor, and an appellate judge—and my assumption of executive power over a fictitious conglomerate was, to them, the least quirky aspect of their assignment. For this project, I had required them to participate in the charade: Each student took on a distinct role within his or her group so that their presentations and papers were "reports" to the company's management from the "creative executive" or the "art director" of each campaign. Following the presentations, each student team submitted its ads along with individually written and revised papers; each student ultimately received a grade that combined the collaborative and the individual elements of the project. Without a doubt, this was a labor-intensive assignment for all of us. It was also one of the most successful class projects in which I've participated.

The assignment was inspired by Chapter 2, "Brought to You B(u)y: The Signs of Advertising" of *Signs of Life*, particularly several articles that I had taught before. Ads are great material for composition classes for many reasons, not least of which are their familiarity to students and the ways in which ads themselves can be examined for a visual "thesis" and "examples." I had assigned earlier classes Jack Solomon's "Masters of Desire: The Culture of American Advertising" (Chapter 2). This article is an excellent model for the mechanics of semiotic analysis, as well as for its presentation of arguments supported by reference to multiple specific examples. In particular, Solomon's article is helpful to students writing papers on advertising. Thomas Hine's "What's in a Package" (from Chapter 1, "Consuming Passions: The Culture of American Consumption") is another article that supports this assignment well.

My earlier classes had discussed these essays in small groups and as a class; we had analyzed ads in small groups and as a class; and eventually, students wrote a paper on ad analysis. This approach was successful, but I had grown tired of my old plan. This time, once my students were familiar with the semiotic approach, I asked them to become ad executives. In groups of five, they were responsible for inventing a consumer product or service and designing a marketing strategy, complete with print and video ads. Along with the ads, each student was to write a five-page paper that referenced the articles in *Signs of Life* to examine his or her particular role in the group project. Although I designed the individual job titles and separated the class into groups of five, students were responsible for assigning each role according to their own interests. This was more than a concession to my love of role-playing assignments; individual paper assignments were determined according to a student's position in the group. Each group had a Creative Executive, who coordinated the presentation and the advertisements with one another; organized students self-selected for this job within minutes of receiving the assignment. The Marketing Manager — usually a budding business major — was responsible for analyzing the target markets of the product and the target audiences of the ads. Public Relations Gurus examined the correspondence among the images of the company as a whole and those projected through the product and the ad campaign. Finally, the Art Director and Video Director took primary responsibility for analyzing the print ad and the video ad, respectively. Most students assumed their roles with great panache: One Marketing Manager promised in his paper that his team's product would "become the flagship brand for the corporation in the twenty-first century," while one Video Director requested my help in lobbying the campus media lab for permission to use their digital editing equipment, above and beyond the assignment's requirements. (The lab approved her request, and the resulting ad for a state-of-the-art health club was stunningly professional.)

I realize that the above constitutes a lot of work for two weeks. Then again, I work at an institution with remarkable technological resources for instructors and undergraduates. My students had free access to video cameras, viewing monitors, analog and digital editing booths, networked computers, color printers, and several different desktop-publishing and photo-editing applications, as well as university employees whose job it is to train and assist undergraduates in using these resources. With hindsight, however, a modified version of this assignment would work, with few adjustments, for students whose multimedia resources extend to a box of magic markers and a piece of paper. The assignment stipulated that no points would be added or subtracted for technological prowess or the lack thereof, and team grades were determined by the creativity and coherence of the ideas behind the advertising campaign rather than by any advanced graphics in the ads themselves. I received an assortment of print ads, including a construction-paper-and-crayon collage, a computer-generated blend of text and scanned images, and one hand-lettered, hand-colored poster board.

I had two goals for this project. Primarily, I hoped to help strengthen students' critical thinking, reading, and writing skills. By putting them in the role of producers, rather than consumers, of popular culture, I hoped that my students would take a more active critical stance toward their subject matter. By requiring a significant amount of teamwork, I multiplied the occasions on which students would examine, critique, or simply discuss their own writing and how to improve it. Beyond merely drilling students in criticism, however, I tried to engage those critical skills on a terrain where the class felt more at ease and more invested than they do with traditional academic analysis. Using *Signs of Life* gave me a head start here: Students are already impressed and excited to be analyzing popular culture—a field that they often feel more authorized to critique than they do others. I deliberately structured the assignment as a "professional" project that employed several different media, in the hope that students might think of composition as more than a dull academic rite of passage and see that clear writing skills have valuable applications in the rest of the world.

In previous composition classes, my students had examined popular culture as critical consumers—but consumers nonetheless. Often, students felt so close to the objects under scrutiny that they had difficulty suspending personal judgments: For example, students who attend class bedecked in Calvin Klein logo attire rarely want to consider the semiotic subtexts of CK advertisements. They want reassurance that they look cool. Alternatively, out of a naive belief that "criticism" as such is inherently negative, some students resist imputing any motive to advertising other than genuine desire to communicate a product's virtues. By imagining themselves as advertisers, my students gained a crucial detachment from their material. Indeed, this is one of the reasons that the editors of *Signs of Life* suggest putting students in the role of advertisers for a day. Not only did my students take advantage of multiple possibilities for building signs into advertisements, but the depth of their subsequent analyses improved once they had recognized how far those signs and sign systems could extend. Because they were responsible for every editorial decision in creating the ads, students quickly dispensed with the obvious images—a smiling trio of women, for example—to focus on countless subtle signals working alongside the obvious. During one class period given over to team strategy, I overheard students arguing about the semiotic importance of the size and color of different typefaces, longer or shorter words in a slogan, the ethnic backgrounds of the people depicted in each ad, and the placement of each element in relation to the others.

Thus the smiling trio of women in one group's print advertisement was meant to signal feminist independence, appropriately enough for the product, which was marketed to women. Yet in the final analysis, the trio was also deliberately multicultural; dressed in casual clothes that bore insignias from prestigious universities; depicted in black and white; seated on comfortable couches; smiling at each other rather than at the camera; in a home and not outdoors or in a bar; surrounded by signs of professional success such as briefcases, cellular phones, and computers; and finally, accompanied by a minimum of discreet advertising copy. Another group, selling sports sunglasses to the college market, designed their ad so that the sunglasses appeared in the center of the page, lit with a spotlight. Through the lighting, which they intended to connote museum exhibits or stage performance, they suggested the elitism, prestige, and attention-getting qualities of their product without including any text to that effect. Once students understood from experience that such signals are at least as important to a successful ad's composition as the depiction of the commodity itself, they ceased making the single most common undergraduate objection to pop culture analysis. In other words, they stopped saying, "It's just an ad. Aren't we reading too much into this?" and directed their energies at designing advertisements and writing their papers.

My students had fun designing their products and advertisements, and they zeroed in on some great marketing opportunities: One group dreamed up "the Air Executive," a comfortable shoe for businessmen, while another spotted an opening in the beverage market and created Belmont Beer for Women, named for Portia's hometown in *The Merchant of Venice.* Their general enthusiasm for the project carried over to their papers, which helped to motivate some extremely productive individual and peer writing conferences. Although I have used several forms of peer review in previous courses, I sometimes fear that it can be a one-sided process. Peer editors have little invested in the outcome of their reviews, other than their desire that a conscientious reading will elicit an equally careful review from their partners. Yet my students tended to grow complacent with or tired of the peer review process over the term, giving cursory attention to the papers of their peers. With this assignment, though, each student's paper was linked to the group's final project. Every student thus had a vested interest in improving his or her teammates' papers, inasmuch as each member's understanding of the team's goals directly affected the group's success. Each student's paper was reviewed by two other teammates, doubling the amount of constructive criticism for each paper and ensuring that the group was in accord regarding the strategy behind the ad campaign.

Without exception, the quality of my students' writing shot up on these papers. Of course, not everyone received an A, but I was able to give the first A that term. Also, for the first time that term, every student received a passing grade on the paper. This was in part due to a significant amount of class time spent discussing the papers and the group project as a whole. During four different class meetings, at least thirty minutes were devoted to team meetings so that students could plan projects and talk about papers, and we spent one entire class peer reviewing drafts. I discovered that students conceived of the project as a whole: During meetings that were technically scheduled for planning presentations, I overheard students brainstorming paper ideas; similarly, students used some of the time intended for essay review to work on video scripts or to discuss the layout of print ads. Because I required every team to meet with me at least once during the planning stages, I could keep track of their progress and offer help wherever needed. Unexpectedly, these mandatory group meetings increased the number of individual student appointments: While reviewing their team project with me, many students signed up for additional one-on-one conferences to discuss their papers. Several students commented to me or on final evaluations that they had never before considered English classes to be that interesting. Such positive feedback was a real thrill on its own but also a gratifying indication that I was successful in achieving my less measurable goals for the project: generating interest in a field that students considered dull or irrelevant and applying student strengths in other fields to composition.

Most of my students were neither English nor humanities majors, and many felt alienated by writing and reading critical essays. Their levels of intimidation ranged from some students' vehement dislike of composition as a practice to the mental block that writing was a born gift and not a teachable skill that improves with practice. By requiring students to work with graphics and video as well as writing, I hoped to tap their creative sides and to uncover dormant talents for alternative forms of composition. One of the great strengths of *Signs of Life* is in its modeling of sophisticated written analysis with everyday objects and media, a feature that tends to make students feel more authorized to critique the material under consideration. I hoped to complement this strategy by combining writing, a skill with which my students did not feel comfortable, with related creative fields where they might feel more at home. Among other things, I discovered that my students excelled at creative multimedia composition, something I wouldn't have known had I assigned only written papers.

Discovering creativity in one area proved helpful in coaching students through other areas. Several students proved to be superb video directors with a natural visual sense of narrative that they were not able to match in their writing. So we started discussing writing on their terms, comparing thesis statements to visual exposition, specific examples to shot composition, and revision to dubbing and editing. I stressed to students that writing, too, is a creative act, even when it is done for academic purposes. Composition skills are not only translatable across different media — from graphic design to written text, say — but are of equal importance in different media for the professional futures of many students. For example, a strong writer will design a Web site better than someone who cannot support a general argument with specific examples. One student, whose level of academic motivation seemed exemplified by his confession (intended, no doubt, as a compliment) that mine was the only class in his schedule that he attended on a regular basis, turned out to be an absolute whiz at video and Web design. His paper, a semiotic analysis of the video ad by the sunglasses group, showcased a previously hidden ability to organize a convincing argument. Like many students, once he wrote about a subject of genuine interest, his writing improved. His argument was an analysis of the episodic nature of the group's ad, which was designed to mimic MTV videos, capitalizing on the short attention spans of the young target market as well as the aura of coolness and sex appeal that MTV projects. His discussion of and evidence for these claims were among the most entertaining, intelligent written work submitted that term.

Along with all of my lofty goals, though, I hoped that this project would help me do what every teacher wants: I wanted to have fun with my class. In this regard, the assignment was an unqualified success. Student presentations and ads were consistently entertaining and intelligent, regardless of the teams' technical prowess. Even the students who borrowed an existing commercial strategy were remarkably canny about the way they chose to do so. By reconfiguring a popular sales pitch to their own product, the student teams were able to reason out the mechanics of how and why particular pitches work. For example, one memorable ad campaign borrowed the "Got Milk?" ad format to sell a college-age dating service. The team was able both to defend the copycat style as a means of investing their service with an aura of wholesomeness, as well as to examine the applicability of the original ad series' signs to their own service, such as the implied urgency in the brief question, the tactic of coming right to the point, and the association of dating with an essential life function. Much more gratifying than the entertainment afforded by such presentations, however, was this project's unexpected effect of forging solidarity among my students, via productive, mutually supportive team relationships that lasted throughout the term. Of course, there was a dysfunctional moment or two — such as a group in which a student defaulted on his or her work or one in which an individual tried to impose his or her personal agenda on the rest of the team. Yet these kinds of glitches, inevitable with any classroom situation involving more than one student, were by far the exception. In each case, difficulty with one individual had the effect of bonding the other members of the team more solidly. With five members to each student team, this still left four people to execute a project, more than enough for successful group work.

I solicited student feedback at all stages of the assignment, reminding them that they were free to offer critiques and make suggestions for improvement, just as I would eventually critique their work. I'd use some of their suggestions if I taught this class again. For one thing, this project was more time-consuming than I had anticipated, for me and for the class. One student suggested simply allowing more than two weeks from start to finish, while another suggested that the video assignment could be modified into a skit forming part of the class presentation, thus saving the time otherwise spent filming and editing. Instead of submitting a video, student groups would turn in their scripts and stage directions. Students also observed that organizing meetings outside of class was difficult for anyone living far from campus. I had randomly assigned students to teams without considering the logistics of their meeting schedules; next time, I'd allow students to organize themselves by geography if that would enable meetings after hours. Finally, it's hard to grade individual students on a group project. Each student justifiably wanted a grade that reflected the work of the individual student, but it can be difficult to separate individual contributions to a group effort. Also justifiably, no student wanted anybody to take credit for work that others had done. My solution was to give each student an average of the group's grade for the project and the individual's grade for the paper. Of course, this had the effect of raising some students' final project grades and lowering others, but there was no case where a student who received a failing grade on the paper received a passing grade for the project. This was the result of luck, not careful planning: Nobody failed the paper. Next time, I'd stipulate that a failing grade on the paper meant a failing grade for that individual on the assignment.

Overall, the advertising project was productive as well as entertaining. I learned along with my students and enjoyed the opportunity to work more closely with them than I usually do: I attended video training sessions with them and held many, many extra office hours to strategize ad campaigns with the different teams or to discuss papers with different students. My one caveat to instructors considering some form of this assignment would be to outdo yourself in offering positive reinforcement. At every stage of the project, I praised the work and the effort that my students were exerting, and our final presentations were followed by a small "Class Clio" ceremony, at which every group and every student received silly awards and certificates for achievements such as "coolest name for a new product," "most likely to turn a huge profit," "ads so hip they're worth taping," and so on. Approximately half the students in my class were first-years, and the rest were split fairly evenly among the upperclassmen, but all of them responded equally well to steady cheerleading.

Ultimately, the true test of a classroom project is the question of whether it is worth repeating. I don't need to think about that one. I'd do it again in a heartbeat—but I'd have to change at least one thing. Next time, I will dispense with the fiction of being Executive Vice President. Next time, I will be CEO.

Chapter 1

CONSUMING PASSIONS

The Culture of American Consumption

We've made consuming behavior the subject of our first chapter in every edition of *Signs of Life* because of the essential role that consumption plays in shaping American popular culture. The culture of consumption is linked most obviously to the topics covered in the first few chapters of *Signs of Life* — that is, cultural products such as advertising, television, and film — but it also affects issues that are raised later in the book, such as the influence of new media and the construction of one's sense of identity. Thus, Chapter 1 serves as an ideal starting point for a course, no matter which other chapters your syllabus includes. You'll also find that beginning with consuming behavior works well because it's part of every student's life, whether your students hail from wealthy suburbs and have lots of disposable income or are working single mothers struggling to make a life for themselves and their families. And it's true for traditional and nontraditional students alike, those entering college straight from high school and those returning after a hiatus. The constant pressure to buy is an unavoidable part of their lives, even if not all are able or willing to respond to that pressure. If you like to start your course by concentrating on personal experience writing, begin with this chapter.

This chapter is also a great place to start if you plan to adopt explicitly the semiotic approach that underlies this text. We've found that semiotics makes immediate sense to students presented in the context of their own behavior. They know, for instance, that they are sending messages to others with their choice of clothing — and they're likely to admit it. Just ask them about the different messages they send when they dress for work, school, or a party. Or ask them how their friends would "read" them differently if they showed up driving an Acura Integra, a Smart car, or a pickup truck. The chapter's introduction emphasizes the link between consumer behavior and one's sense of personal identity to show students that, in a sense, they've been semioticians all along.

The "Discussing the Signs of Consumer Culture" exercise, which asks the class to list and interpret their own clothing styles, is a great icebreaker for the first few days of the term, when students may not know each other and may be a bit shy about talking in class. Note that the exercise encourages students to distinguish between their own interpretations of their clothing and that of others. This distinction between personal and public meanings is important as students learn that academic writing is not simply an assertion of opinion but an expression of opinion through socially constituted discourse conventions. This exercise additionally raises the distinction between the functional and cultural meanings of an object. Students often are willing to challenge another student's claim that, for instance, she wears her ripped blue jeans "just because they're comfortable." Someone in the class inevitably will point out that ripped jeans can cost over a hundred dollars or that they project a cool image, and so on.

Students may be somewhat more resistant to the issue raised in the "Exploring the Signs of Consumer Culture" question, which asks them to reflect on the importance of consumer products in their lives. Because Americans still cling to the belief that one's identity is a highly individualized matter of soul and spirit, it's understandable that students may reject the claim, made explicitly in the Introduction and implicitly in many of the readings, that "you are what you consume." Ask students to share their responses in class, and use them to trigger a discussion of the relative importance of consumer objects and other matters in their lives. You might want to return to this question later in the term, especially after covering some of the selections later in the book that show how American culture often commodifies serious issues. It would be particularly interesting to do so after discussing Chapter 7, "My Selfie, My Self: Ma(s)king Identity in the New Millennium." As this chapter discusses, gender and race are deeply connected to one's sense of personal identity and selfhood, and both are increasingly being appropriated to peddle everything from clothing to universities (check your college catalog for calculated images of multiculturalism).

The "Reading Consumer Culture Online" exercise should allow your students to have some fun interpreting the mythology of American consumerism. You can ask them to explore home-shopping networks and auction Web sites either individually or in small groups; they can visit the addresses suggested in the exercise, but by all means invite them to explore other sites as well. Students may not be instinctively analytical when visiting these sites, because shopping is such a common behavior. So you might prepare them by asking them to look at the products advertised (are they necessities? luxuries?), the images used to make those products seem desirable, and particularly, the target market (typically women). If you ask your whole class to complete this exercise, try assigning small groups a different site, and then ask your students to compare their findings in class. One final note: This exercise works perfectly with the Anne Norton selection.

The chapter covers a range of consumer objects and behaviors, and if pressed for time you could focus on the ones you feel your students could easily relate to. The selection by Laurence Shames provides a general framework for analyzing consumerism — it relates American frontier history to our desire for more goods and services — and thus can be useful no matter which other readings you assign. For two paired selections that focus on consumer behavior, assign both Malcolm Gladwell, who explores how a retail store's design influences consumer behavior, and Anne Norton, who argues that shopping malls and catalogs operate as sign systems designed to stimulate consumption. Stephanie Clifford and Quentin Hardy's essay on retailers' surveillance of our cell phones provides an almost creepy complement to the Gladwell essay. A suite of selections addresses different categories of consumer objects that are all semiotically rich in significance. Jon Mooallem explores how one's items stashed in a lowly self-storage unit, now ubiquitous across America, reveals one's personality, values, and even family history, and Thomas Hine studies a part of everyday life that's often overlooked in academic study — the semiotics of packages. James Roberts next ponders why the plethora of consumer goods available to us today doesn't always seem to make us happy. Phyllis M. Japp and Debra K. Japp discuss the commodification of nature, a marketing device all the more prominent in the now slightly green second decade of the twenty-first century, and Steve McKevitt explores the difference between our "needs" and "wants," finding that too often consumers make no distinction between the two. The chapter concludes with Thomas Frank's analysis of a current marketing trend: the use of countercultural motifs and values to peddle mass-market products that are, in fact, anything but countercultural.

LAURENCE SHAMES

The More Factor (p. 80)

Shames attacks a cherished American myth — that the U.S.A. is a land of endless opportunity — so be prepared for some real opposition to his thesis. Because many students are attending college precisely so that they can expand their opportunities, they hardly want to hear that their hunger for more may not be nourished. Their response may also be complicated if they are recent immigrants whose lives have been directly shaped by this myth or if their families have been hit hard by the ongoing Great Recession. In class, you might focus initially on the first part of Shames's essay, his discussion of the frontier myth of limitless opportunity. Your students are likely to be familiar with this myth from popular media; they could brainstorm examples of TV shows and films that perpetuate this myth. You could ask them to analyze the "Credit Card Barbie" photo on p. 101. In what ways does Barbie — a consumer product herself, of course — both symbolize and encourage consumption among her fans of mostly young girls? Then move to the more troubling of Shames's assertions, his claim that America is "running out of more." This selection was published in 1989, so you could ask your class whether the current economic disaster, which has reached world proportions, has altered the "hunger for more." If your students are all first-years, they might not yet be thinking about job prospects after they graduate from college, but you might ask your class about them anyway. If you have adult students, try sparking a conversation between them and their younger counterparts, who may have had less experience in the working world. Politically conservative students might object that Shames questions the efficacy of a free-market economy, and they'd be right: It's just that Shames would see free-market ideology as problematic. You can complicate Shames's argument by introducing issues of race and gender, given that the opportunities Shames describes have not always been equally available to everyone in America.

This selection is particularly good for teaching critical reading and summarizing skills. The "Reading the Text" questions ask students to identify some of the key concepts in this essay; you could use these exercises to gauge quickly how well your students have grasped Shames's ideas. The first "Reading the Signs" question asks students to ponder the relevance that Shames's thesis has in the twenty-first century; for this prompt, you might invite students to generate evidence both from personal experience and observation and from current political events. Because question 2 points to what is perhaps Shames's most controversial claim — that ethical standards have been destroyed by the hunger for more — it is ideal for staging an in-class debate. In preparing for a debate, students will need to anticipate counterarguments and develop specific evidence; be sure to allot sufficient time, either in or outside of class, for them to do this in groups. You may also want to combine a debate with a discussion of library research techniques (students could investigate, for instance, some of the scandals surrounding Enron, Countrywide, General Motors, BP, and a host of Wall Street inside-traders, most of whom were never prosecuted). Of course, you could change question 2 to an at-home essay as well. The remaining questions ask students to relate this selection to other issues raised in the text. Question 3 is straightforward, asking students to apply Shames's argument to Steve McKevitt's essay in this chapter: How does Shames illuminate our understanding of the sort of consumption cornucopia that McKevitt discusses? Question 4 is more challenging and open-ended, for it asks students whether the hunger for more is quintessentially American or a more universal human trait.

ANNE NORTON

The Signs of Shopping (p. 87)

You can have a lot of fun with Norton's essay: It's a rich analysis of something most people take for granted — shopping malls and catalogs — and it is a perfect complement to Malcolm Gladwell's selection on store design. The article begins in a somewhat dense academic style, but that style diminishes as the article progresses. No matter what your students' economic background, you can assume they're familiar with some sort of mall and occasionally peruse catalogs. Norton's selection works well early in the term, for it provides a wonderful opportunity for combining discussion of personal experience with an analytic interpretation of an accessible topic. Some students may resist Norton's claim that one's behavior can be so thoroughly manipulated by marketers, but ask them to consider specific examples that are close to their own experiences. Why do Victoria's Secret shops feature gilded and lacy touches? What's the image projected by that slick Gap storefront? Some students eagerly embrace Norton's suggestion that malls appeal to women's desire for independence and escape from home; others balk at it. If they do, ask them to test her assertion empirically by performing a rough demographic survey at a local mall. What do their results suggest about the gender patterns in malls?

The "Reading the Text" questions will enable you to see whether students grasp Norton's central concepts or if they have difficulty with her occasionally academic style; they will also reveal if your students hesitate to accept her premise that an everyday activity such as shopping can be constrained by political ideologies and cultural mythologies. If they do resist this premise, ask them whether they respond differently when visiting, say, an Urban Outfitters store versus a Wal-Mart—and why. In varying ways, the Reading the Signs questions ask students to apply or extend Norton's argument about shopping. Question 1 asks them to apply Norton's claims to window displays in a local mall; this question works especially well if they study the displays of at least two shops, preferably shops intended for the same market. In doing so, students will quickly pick up on the consistent signs sent for the market, as long as they overlook superficial differences. Question 2 should trigger a great in-class discussion, with students comparing catalogs in small groups. (For variety, you could bring in some catalogs you receive, and before the assignment you might make some catalogue requests online for less mainstream companies.) Expect that many students will bring in Victoria's Secret and Abercrombie and Fitch catalogues. Question 5 is a companion essay question that invites students to analyze closely one catalogue. Question 3 is ambitious, for it invites students to test Norton's gender-based argument by interviewing women of different ages. For this question, you might first want the class to discuss interviewing strategies—and the importance of interpreting an interviewee's comments. Questions 4 and 6 turn to the Internet, with question 4 asking students to study the Home Shopping Network or a similar program and question 6 focusing their attention on a commercial Web site. This last one, we've found, proves to be particularly eye opening to those students who tend to take anything and everything they see online for granted. Expect a lot of comments to the effect that "it's so convenient that X store's website enables me to assemble a complete outfit just with a few clicks of a button." Of course.

MALCOLM GLADWELL

The Science of Shopping (p. 93)

This essay, paired with Anne Norton's selection, provides an in-depth look at the ways marketing techniques deliberately manipulate consumer behavior—a topic we've always found energizes (and sometimes angers) students. Gladwell gives a detailed description of the ways retailers use spatial design to subtly coerce consumers to buy. Whether your students are city folk or suburbanites, well off or struggling to make ends meet, you can assume that they're familiar with malls and chain stores like The Gap (which Gladwell discusses) and that their consuming behavior has been affected by retail design. Thus this selection provides a good opportunity for combining personal experience with an analysis of a topic accessible to all students. Some students may resist the notion that one's behavior can be shaped by a store's layout and other physical cues, but remind them that this is the assumption that successful retailers make—it's not just Gladwell's opinion. Indeed, Gladwell focuses on Paco Underhill, a retailers' anthropologist who studies consumer behavior. If students don't believe Underhill's advice to retailers has an effect, ask them to consider retailing patterns: Why do stores almost always locate the sale section in the back? Why do college bookstores locate popular trade books, bestsellers, and merchandise such as calendars and campus-themed gewgaws up front, near the cash registers, and relegate the required textbooks to the back? Have your students ever bought an unnecessary item because of this arrangement? For more on Underhill's strategies, consult the Web site for Envirosell, his behavioral market research and consulting company (www.envirosell.com). We link Gladwell's essay with Anne Norton's because despite a slightly different focus, both investigate the ways marketers use signs to shape consumers' behavior and consumption choices.

In varying ways, the "Reading the Signs" questions ask students to apply or respond to Gladwell's observations about the strategies for customer manipulation. Question 1 asks students to apply Gladwell's points to specific examples such as a supermarket or chain store. For this topic, we've had students form teams and visit the store together as a group brainstorming exercise; each team presents its findings to the class. Some national chain stores that work very well are Victoria's Secret, Urban Outfitters, Whole Foods, and Abercrombie and Fitch (we've had A&F employees reveal that they receive explicit instructions to use many of the same techniques that Gladwell describes). Such field observation can train students to attend to detail; you might just warn them that some store managers might not appreciate it if students take photographs without prior permission (so they need to be careful with that phone camera!). A variant is question 3, which has them visit the Web site of a major retailer and study how the virtual space encourages them to buy. This topic can be challenging, for students may see some features of the Web site as mere functional conveniences (e.g., the "shopping carts" that allow you to pile up merchandise as you're "browsing" through the store) that, although helpful to the virtual shopper, also stimulate additional consumption (it's easy to forget how much you've stashed in your virtual cart). Your students may be disturbed by the invasion of personal privacy that's implicit in some of Underhill's techniques; if that's the case, they may enjoy the class debate on the ethics of retail anthropology suggested in question 2. (Stephanie Clifford and Quentin Hardy's selection in this chapter could help with this topic.) Finally, question 4 invites students to respond to Gladwell's question, "Should we be afraid of Paco Underhill?" (para. 18). Be sure students note that although at times Gladwell seems to suggest that the answer is yes, ultimately he decides that it is the shoppers who manipulate the retailers—a debatable point given his evidence.

JON MOOALLEM

The Self-Storage Self (p. 102)

It's often said that the boxes and plastic bags stuffed away in our closets and garages can reveal thousands of tales of our lives, personalities, quarrels, crises, and triumphs. And that commonplace is indeed true, as our possessions, even those discarded or ignored, do tell a narrative about our lives. But what about the items we hold on to, even though we might not have space for them? They can reveal just as much, even more. In this accessible essay, Mooallem explores the world of self-storage: an unusual topic in a composition textbook, we know! But he offers a fascinating insight into what our possessions — prized, hidden, loathed — say about us individually and as a culture. If you have any students smirk at the idea of self-storage units as being "low class" (or if you feel that way yourself), consider Mooallem's description of the veritable explosion of this business in the last decade. Much of that has to do with the Great Recession, of course, and people's displacement from their jobs and homes and families. But it also reveals something about Americans' regard for possessions, goods, stuff: We tend to keep it all because, somehow, without it a part of us gets lost. If your students doubt this, think about how people cope when a natural disaster destroys their home. If they are able to salvage anything, what takes priority? If they can't, how do they respond to the loss?

Our "Reading the Signs" questions start with a journal entry that asks students to examine their (and/or their family's) attitudes toward their possessions, prompting them to imagine how they might "triage" their stuff given a financial or other emergency. Ask them to go beyond the obvious first choices: important documents and photographs. If they do, then the question will prove revealing to them. Our next two questions, both framed as essay prompts, connect Mooallem's article to other selections in this chapter. Question 2 pulls out a quote from the article that equates having material goods with an American identity; the question sends students to Lawrence Shames's article and to the chapter introduction for help in plumbing this claim. With a somewhat different focus, question 3 asks students to read Mooallem's article in light of the assumption Steve McKevitt makes in his essay that America's love for consumer goods has led to environmental damage. If you have students interested in green issues, this topic will get them involved. Question 4 departs somewhat from the focus on possessions themselves and invites students to debate one of the claims made by an interviewee from this article, about the future of the American economy. Here, the focus of the prompt is on argumentative strengths and weaknesses, and thus it is good for a close rhetorical reading of a claim.

STEPHANIE CLIFFORD AND QUENTIN HARDY

Attention, Shoppers: Store Is Tracking Your Cell (p. 110)

This selection is quick and easy, yet it provides a valuable complement to the Malcolm Gladwell and Anne Norton selections in this chapter, as it updates the recent ways retailers use technology to track, mark, and target their consumers. Check your i-Phone while inside Nordstrom? Gotcha. Or even your local coffee boutique? Gotcha. Even though most of us know that Google (and others) sell our personal information all the time, a lot of consumers assume that, when they walk into a store, they are not under surveillance (except by the anti-shoplifting kind, of course). But surveillance has come a long way from just preventing thieves; it now acts as an aggressive marketing tool, hidden behind the cloak of "convenience" that really means manipulation. Imagine the response of one student who thought, "Hey, I just heard that the store has a one-hour sale on bras! Gotta check it out!" And then she bought two bras she didn't really need at a price that wasn't really all that great a deal. While your students might have fun getting a quickie coupon when they enter a store, this selection should remind them of one of our fundamental semiotic principles: "Don't take things at face value."

This reading is ideal for assignments early in the term that require less complicated explication. Our first "Reading the Signs" question asks students to explore, in their journals or reading logs, why such retail surveillance of their phone use is "creepy." You could also just raise this question in class; be sure to ask students to define what constitutes "creepiness" for them. Question 2 goes beyond the personal to the institutional, prompting students to compare brick-and-mortar outlets' surveillance techniques with those of on-line retailers (which sometimes are negligible, sometimes extreme). To develop their arguments on this topic, students might read carefully some of those on-line privacy disclosures from various retailers, all that tiny print most consumers don't read before they hit "accept" because the reading would postpone the purchase of that jacket, e-toy, or whatever. For a more challenging problem, try question 3, which connects this selection to Malcolm Gladwell's article and asks for a more contemplative argument about the ethical problems that retail surveillance, of whatever sort, might pose. We fear that many today would not see any ethical problems because "everyone is doing it," and besides, anything "electronic is cool." We hope your students prove us wrong.

THOMAS HINE

What's in a Package (p. 113)

At first, students view packages as purely functional: They hold toothpaste or deodorant or whatever. But Hine should open their eyes to the images packages create for their products. His selection is easy to read, and students are likely to be persuaded *and* fascinated by his discussion both of the marketing decisions behind package design (why are billions spent on packaging, anyway?) and of the cultural differences in packaging. Ask your students about trends in packaging design. Why, for instance, was one variety of Oral-B dental floss available in a translucent aqua package reminiscent of an iMac? Why did Pepsi's diet soda "skinny can" flop? Whether your students accept Hine's notions, you can plan a great session by assigning "Reading the Signs" question 1, which asks students to bring a product to class. We've suggested that students bring items from the same product category to allow for comparison of design choices. As an alternative, you might identify four or five categories and have small groups of students sign up for each. If you ask students to give brief presentations of their object, be sure to give them a strict time limit (two or three minutes) so that all students have a chance to present. Questions 2 and 4 are similar in that they invite students to analyze the packaging of one retail outlet (with question 4 specifying an outlet with an explicit political theme). You can stage in-class activities, similar to those called for in question 1, by asking your students to bring to class samples of the packaging from their store. Questions 3 and 5 relate the issue to students' own consuming behaviors. Question 3 calls for a journal entry on the appeal of packaging, and question 5 asks students to interpret, through a stranger's eyes, the packages visible in their own home. Jon Mooallem's essay in this chapter is a natural complement to Hine's selection and can help students respond.

JAMES A. ROBERTS

The Treadmill of Consumption (p. 123)

Why does owning consumer products make us happy? Or, not owning them make us unhappy? Or, owning them also make us unhappy? Roberts explores the psychological value of our possessions, especially when they can perform as exhibits of "conspicuous consumption." Roberts mentions some products that are not likely to be among those that typical-age college students covet or even know about (Patek Philippe watches, $2,000 fountain pens). And thus some might deny that they buy items to be happy because, of course, they are college students and don't have tons of disposable income. But even among students, some products earn more social cache than others. And Robert's point that "no consumer product category has been left untouched" by the desire for status consumption would be a response to that denial. Roberts's opening discussion of cell phones is a case in point. Ask your class what they like pulling out of a bag (a gold i-Phone 5 these days) and what they would be embarrassed to show to their friends (a flip phone). Why? What degree of happiness might the former provide? Other product categories that students might relate to include shoes (especially athletic shoes) or jeans or a handbag, video games, and virtually any electronic toy or device.

Our "Reading the Signs" questions range from the personal to the semiotic. The first question asks students to explore what constitutes consumer status symbols within their own circle of friends and how owning such an item (or not owning it) might affect their sense of happiness. If a student wants to argue that he or she really doesn't care about the status value of possessions, that is fine. Ask this student to contemplate why he or she may have been able to avoid the status symbol fetish that is so common. Roberts's conclusion is rather sober, as he fears that the treadmill of consumption will only start running faster and faster; question 2 sends students to two selections, by Lawrence Shames and Steve McKevitt, to evaluate Roberts's concerns. Our third question switches to media analysis, asking students to use Robert's arguments as a critical framework to analyze a consumerist-themed TV show, especially a reality TV program like *Keeping Up with the Kardashians*. If we're lucky, by the time this edition of *Signs of Life* is available, that program will not longer be broadcast. But we are sure that plenty of alternatives will be available for student analysis.

PHYLLIS M. JAPP AND DEBRA K. JAPP

Purification Through Simplification: Nature, the Good Life, and Consumer Culture (p. 128)

This is a fairly long and complex article, so it's an ideal choice if you want to teach your students critical reading strategies, conventions of academic writing, or simply ways to master a more complicated, theoretically based argument. Because the writing is relatively straightforward, your students could work on those issues without having to wade through waist-deep academese. It is also a good choice if you are interested in using Kenneth Burke's ideas in your class, as Japp and Japp use Burkean rhetoric as their critical framework for analyzing the tension between Americans' professed desire for simplicity and environmental consciousness and the decidedly commercial commodity culture in which we live. If you want the class to adopt a Burkean perspective, you'd do well to assign a prewriting exercise in which they summarize his theory of symbolic action and then discuss their summaries in class, so you can address any confusion ("Reading the Text" question 2 suggests this). This will give you an opportunity to discuss the extent to which academic analysis is based on a theoretical foundation; you could have your students walk through the essay's introduction to Burke the scholar, then its explanation of basic Burkean principles and their application to the essay's primary object of analysis. The authors focus their analysis on the cable show *The Good Life*, which, though no longer in production, is available on various online TV archives. You'd do well to make available to students at least one of the show's episodes so you can discuss it in detail in class, whether or not you emphasize the theoretical underpinnings of the argument. Should your students doubt that the voluntary simplicity ethos that Japp and Japp describe is still in force, show them an issue of *Real Simple*—a perfect current instance of the contradictions that the essay exposes.

And that is exactly why we've included this article in *Signs of Life*. Americans' presumed love of the "great outdoors," the related commodification of nature itself by the tourist and travel industries, and the less-related exploitation of nature to market a "good life" that is anything but natural is a complicated and, to us at least, painful clash between some of our most fundamental ideologies. You will be able to create challenging, provocative assignments based on this reading. Our first two "Reading the Signs" questions are simple and direct: Question 1 asks students to analyze an episode of *The Good Life* to test one of the essay's major assertions; question 2 has them analyze a magazine like *Real Simple* or a similarly themed TV show. A related theme in question 6 has them study *Martha Stewart Living*, a rather pure instance of a "visual drama of the good life." A rather different challenge is posed by question 3, which asks students to analyze Jon Krakauer's *Into the Wild* as a possible fable of an experiment in voluntary simplicity. Expect students to be caught up in the romanticism of the loner figure who professes that he wants simply to commune with nature. As Krakauer's book illustrates (although the author does not make this argument), a lot of self-promotion can be seen in the protagonist's actions; be sure students take that into account in whatever argument they assert. This selection works well in a unit on advertising, particularly so-called green advertising. Accordingly, question 4 sends students to Julia Corbett's article in Chapter 2 to examine green ads in light of the tensions Japp and Japp outline, and question 5 asks them to compare the voluntary simplicity movement with the countercultural poses analyzed by Thomas Frank in "Commodify Your Dissent." For this latter assignment, students should focus on how faux nature and faux revolution occupy so much of contemporary advertising.

STEVE McKEVITT

Everything Now (p. 143)

A complement to James A. Roberts's "The Treadmill of Consumption," McKevitt's selection offers a trenchant analysis of the difference between our needs as consumers and our wants. You might find most useful McKevitt's discussion of A. H. Maslow's "hierarchy of needs." First published in 1943, it still provides a compelling schema for understanding human motivation. Ask your students: How would they define their own "needs" in each of Maslow's categories? To what extent are those needs satisfied? If not, do they belong in the category of "wants"? We suggest such questions because young people — those of typical college age — sometimes substitute a want (for a nonconsumerist example, a 1:00 p.m. class) for a need (a class that satisfied their writing requirement). When the only open sections for that class are at 8:00 a.m., the distinction between the two categories starts to collide. If you have a diverse age group in your class, you might want to trigger a discussion of how one's experiential demographic (e.g., eighteen-year-old right out of high school or twentysomething returning to college after spending time in the military or middle-aged single mom) can affect one's definition of needs and wants.

We should note that although McKevitt includes some data from his native country, England, he extends his comments to Western culture more generally, especially to American culture. An interesting line of inquiry might be whether the "everything now" mentality that McKevitt outlines has, thanks to globalization, become prominent in other nations. Here international students can provide revealing contributions to the discussion. Another line relates to McKevitt's concluding remarks concerning climate change; for an environmental edge to your discussion of consumerism, see the Roberts and Japp and Japp articles in this chapter, as well as the Julia Corbett piece in Chapter 2.

The first "Reading the Signs" question is a journal prompt asking students to respond to one of McKevitt's key points about whether consumer goods can make one happy. Of course, this question could also be a great way to jump-start class discussion of the topic. For a more focused class exercise, consider the second question, which invites the class to brainstorm their "needs" and "wants," and then analyze the collective lists. Here we suggest that (if possible) you collect students' lists anonymously and write them on the board, so that no one feels embarrassed about his or her revelations. Alternatively, if yours is an online classroom, you might use a chat or discussion forum that keeps writers' identities anonymous. Today, among the products that students declare high on the "need" list include electronic devices, from laptops and tablets to iPhones and many other toys. For a more academic essay, question 3 sends students to the research study described in the Chapter 5 article "Students Addicted to Social Media." With this question, consumption, overconsumption, and one's sense of "need" all collide with interesting ramifications. This truly is a question with no "correct answer"! Finally, a more focused question 4 asks students to update and analyze the claims the McKevitt makes about one consumer product, bottled water. You could also assign the Thomas Hine article from this chapter about packaging.

THOMAS FRANK

Commodify Your Dissent (p. 150)

In this selection, Frank takes aim at one of today's dominant marketing techniques, the use of countercultural imagery to peddle everything from burgers to men's cologne (hardly revolutionary products!). Most students should be able to understand Frank's language, but they may not all be clued into some of his cultural references; students born in the 1990s may not be able to connect with names like Jerry Rubin and Jesse Helms or even Alan Ginsberg. Before discussing this essay, you could ask students (individually or in pairs) to list unfamiliar cultural references and then research them on the Internet; the whole class can then share their findings. You might also spend some time reviewing the Beat Generation and examining what role the Beats play in Frank's argument. The use of countercultural imagery as a marketing tool is hardly new (you might recall Nike's controversial adoption of the Beatles' "Revolution" in the late 1980s), but it seems endemic right now, and thus it's unlikely that students will balk at Frank's basic premise. They may, however, provide the circular explanation that these styles, and the larger image they project, are just "cool." If they do, try to get them to probe further: *Why* is it cool to look defiant and rebellious? Is one really being rebellious when the products that create that image are mass-produced and mass marketed? What would constitute a "genuine" countercultural idea?

And you can challenge them with some current examples. Case in point: the widespread use of Shepard Fairey's poster "Hope" created for the 2008 Barack Obama presidential campaign. How many products still carry this image, ranging from posters to T-shirts, to "fine art" (students may not know about that)? In what ways does commodification of an ideological position enhance it? Detract from it? Demean it? These are all questions that students might want to consider.

Frank's selection lends itself to assignments and activities that ask students to interpret popular media products. "Reading the Signs" question 1 asks them to study a current magazine, or other advertising source, to determine whether the cultural rebel remains a marketing motif. Question 2 broadens the issue by having the class brainstorm current media figures who sport the rebel attitude in preparation for individual essays on what the popularity of these figures says about modern American culture. Expect students to draw upon the music industry (especially hip-hop, but not exclusively that segment) and the film industry (for its abundance of bad-boy and bad-girl stars). Justin Bieber and Lindsey Lohan might top their lists, but you could ask your class to range beyond these two sorry-sorts. (Yes, you may note an editorial comment here that you can feel free to ignore.) More challenging is question 3, which has students take on Frank's claim that marketing exploits the values of individualism rather than promoting conformity. For a broad-scale analytic assignment, have students try question 4, in which they visit a youth-oriented store and analyze whether it uses any of the countercultural motifs Frank discusses. We suggest you have students visit shops such as Urban Outfitters or Diesel, as they fit the pattern Frank describes. To heighten their critical response to a store that they might be (too) familiar with, you might first discuss Thomas Hine's "What's in a Package" and Malcolm Gladwell's "The Science of Shopping," both in this chapter. This assignment is ideal for a group project, as individuals can focus on one aspect of the store (advertising, packaging, mannequins, etc.) and the group can present its collective observations and interpretations to the class. For a more narrow focus, try question 5, which asks students to test Frank's claims about the imagery embraced by modern business by analyzing either a current business magazine or a corporate website.

Chapter 2

BROUGHT TO YOU B(U)Y

The Signs of Advertising

Advertising has long been a favorite topic in composition classes, and for good reason. Students can write critically about visual texts that affect their everyday lives and that therefore seem more accessible than written texts. In this chapter, we ask students to go beyond the usual evaluative criticism of advertising to an assessment of how ads not only reflect but also shape American culture. We've chosen readings that do not simply interpret ads but also address the ways advertising uses fundamental American mythologies to shape a consumerist ideology. It's unlikely that students have encountered such a perspective in high school (where they also may have discussed advertising), so you can look forward to introducing them to a fresh angle on the subject. If you're emphasizing a semiotic approach, we strongly recommend covering this chapter, for ads are natural for semiotic analysis. If you're skirting semiotics, you can still use these selections, as they can trigger careful, close readings of advertising texts, no matter what the methodology. Students take to analyzing advertising quite readily, so you should encounter little or no resistance to this topic. Indeed, you and your class should have some fun with it!

Your students will need little preparation for discussing advertising because it's such a familiar part of their lives, but they may need some guidance in talking critically and precisely about it. Providing such guidance is the aim of the "Discussing the Signs of Advertising" exercise, which asks that students each bring an ad to class and discuss their interpretations of it in small groups. You may want to review first the follow-up questions in the exercise; they are intended to help students move beyond evaluative judgments to a critical analysis of how ads work. We suggest that, as students discuss their ads, you move from group to group, pushing them to be ever more precise and analytic. If you have time, ask students in each group to select one ad and present their interpretation to the whole class. The "Exploring the Signs of Advertising" exercise stimulates students' critical thinking in a different way: It asks them to create their own alternative ad and then assess their creation. Putting students in the advertiser's seat, we hope, will enable them to see how the complex rhetoric of advertising is constituted. This exercise works best if you suggest that students redesign an ad they don't like because of its ideology. It's not a problem if students have trouble coming up with a new design; in such cases, they could then reflect on the tenacious hold advertising images have on our imaginations and worldviews. We've made this a journal topic, but it certainly could be a more formal assignment. The "Reading Advertising Online" exercise asks students to visit *Advertising Age*'s Web site for its compendium of Super Bowl ads (or find the ads on YouTube). This question is meant to get students to consider how advertising has become a source of entertainment in its own right; after all, many viewers watch the Super Bowl to check out the ads, not the sports, and many ads come with their own pre-broadcast media hype.

When constructing assignments involving advertising, be sure to require students to attach to their essays copies of print or Internet ads they may be interpreting (or to make sure that the URL for a video ad is reliable); otherwise, you might have trouble evaluating their work. Students can benefit if, early in the drafting stage, you review basic advertising terms, such as *copy* and *layout*. This will enable students to avoid clunky phrasing like "the words that appear in the advertisement" or "the way the images are arranged in the ad." You don't need to supply a lot of ad-biz jargon, but a few precise terms will yield stronger essays.

This chapter approaches advertising from a wide range of perspectives. It starts with Jack Solomon's argument that a fundamental American ideology is revealed in advertising's paradoxical adoption of elitist and populist appeals, a position that provides a clear critical framework that students find extremely accessible. Two paired readings follow, by James B. Twitchell and Steve Craig, respectively, both examining how advertisers essentially create images for consumers. Twitchell exposes the very precise stereotypical categories marketers use to target consumers, and Craig offers a broad-based consideration of how advertising relies on specific gender roles that it helps perpetuate. Continuing the gender focus, Jennifer Pozner explores the contradictory responses to Dove's "Real Beauty" ad campaign, which employs unconventionally "normal" models in the service of some very conventional beauty products. We include an inside look at how the advertising business operates: Gloria Steinem exposes the surprisingly cozy relationship between advertising and journalism in the magazine industry. Juliet B. Schor's "Selling to Children: The Marketing of Cool" is an eye-opening exposé of how advertisers create a cool and edgy image to hook child and teen consumers. Joseph Turow provides his own exposé of online consumer profiling and surveillance. A reading on so-called green advertising by Julia B. Corbett follows. Closing the chapter, the Portfolio of Ads presents sample ads that you can use for class discussion or essay assignments. If you plan to use just a few selections, many of them pair up well with other themes. If your course focuses on gender, for instance, the Steve Craig, Jennifer Pozner, and Gloria Steinem articles are essential readings. If you're interested in critiquing the behind-the-scenes techniques used to stimulate consumer desire, the readings by Schor, Steinem, and Twitchell complement the Chapter 1 readings by Gladwell, Clifford, and Hardy.

JACK SOLOMON

Masters of Desire: The Culture of American Advertising (p. 166)

This essay is one of *Signs of Life*'s favorites because of its clear, engaging examination of two dominant and conflicting mythologies underlying American advertising: populism and elitism. Your students should easily grasp the clear paradox that Solomon outlines; for that reason, this essay is ideal for analytic essays that ask students to apply this paradox to advertisements they have selected. "Reading the Signs" question 3 has students do just that as an in-class exercise; your students should bring a popular magazine to class, and in small groups or whole-class discussion, identify the patterns they detect in the advertising. A simpler exercise would have each student bring to class one advertisement that is overtly populist or elitist. One at a time, students quickly categorize their ad and give a brief explanation, or small groups could analyze their ads. It's interesting to see which category predominates. If students complain that the ads that Solomon mentions are dated (this essay was first published in 1988), challenge them to analyze their own current examples in today's political context (the task required by question 1). We've noticed that these appeals are most commonly used in media that target a wide audience (not surprisingly, because such an audience is more likely to hold mainstream American values); a twist to this question would ask students to compare ads in general interest magazines and those intended for specialized readerships. For an essay that focuses on the class implications of the paradox Solomon describes, assign question 2. If you're encouraging your students to take a historical view, assign question 5, which asks them to compare advertising appeals from earlier decades with those used today. As you explain this topic to your students, encourage them to go beyond describing the differences and similarities they see to analyzing the values and mythologies that underlie the ads. Question 4 addresses a broader issue: It asks the class to brainstorm a list of status symbols and then study the nature of their appeal; this topic would make a successful essay assignment as well. A corollary article would be James Roberts's "The Treadmill of Consumption" in Chapter 1.

JAMES B. TWITCHELL

What We Are to Advertisers (p. 177)

Twitchell's selection pairs with the following reading by Steve Craig, as both explore how advertisers create identities, and very traditional ones, for consumers. Twitchell explains how advertisers presume different market segments share similar values and mindsets and then use these values and mindsets to manipulate consumers. Sounds like stereotyping? It is, but it's based not on social convention, but on supposedly scientific research (you be the judge). You can initially have some fun with Twitchell, as most readers instinctively are tempted to see where they would be slotted in the Values and Lifestyle System (VALS), a scheme marketers use to correlate consumer values, belief systems, personality profile, and financial resources. In which categories do your students or their families fit? Are there any patterns in the class's responses? Note that because students may have to reveal financial background, you'd do well to keep your survey informal and voluntary. ("Reading the Signs" question 1 has students write a journal entry in which they locate themselves in the VALS and respond to doing so.) But you'll want to move quickly from trying out the VALS paradigm to the larger issues it raises. What are its limitations? Does it neglect some consumer groups? VALS does not make explicit ethnicity or gender as criteria, but are ethnic and gender identities presumed? If so, what difference does that make? Do students see larger consequences in a multibillion-dollar industry relying heavily on narrowly drawn social stereotypes? As Twitchell acknowledges, such categorization of consumers seems to be an effective selling tool. What does that suggest about the power of marketing campaigns not simply to get us to buy but also to adjust our behaviors, even our values, to social norms?

Because Twitchell makes unambiguous claims here, students should have no problem responding to his essay. "Reading the Signs" question 2 allows students to address the question of whether the VALS paradigm accurately predicts consumer behavior; to generate evidence for this topic, students might conduct surveys of acquaintances' habits as consumers. Questions 3 and 4 solicit argumentative essays: Question 3 invites students to analyze the values implicit in VALS itself, and question 4 asks students to use the VALS paradigm in an analysis of the interviewees Jon Mooallem describes in "The Self-Storage Self" (Chapter 1). Question 5 sends students to the Malcolm Gladwell, Stephanie Clifford, and Quentin Hardy selections in Chapter 1, to argue whether the research techniques described in these readings, which are often based on personal information or surveillance, are ethical.

STEVE CRAIG

Men's Men and Women's Women (p. 182)

Gender often is construed as a "women's issue," and to combat that misconception we include Craig's essay, which addresses advertising directed at both women and men. If your class is focusing on gender, Craig's selection is a must-read that students should find accessible. Craig begins by outlining the advertising technique of demographic targeting (you might want to read this selection along with James B. Twitchell's piece in this chapter) as well as the assumptions advertisers make about both genders that drive their creation of rather traditional identities for consumers. Craig then turns to four commercials that serve as examples of how men and women are portrayed to their own gender and to the other. You can have some fun with this selection, asking students first to debate Craig's interpretation of the ads ("Reading the Signs" question 1 invites students to do just that). You might divide the class into four groups and assign each one of Craig's categories; have students analyze magazines for their category. What kind of publication tends to have "men's men" ads? What kinds have "women's men" ads? What do their results suggest about the publications' assumptions about their readership? Another exercise that can yield lively discussion is to review the categories, and then use them to group a random collection of ads that include both male and female models (you might bring to class, say, twenty ads taken from magazines for both genders). Which categories dominate, and why?

This selection lends itself to a variety of analytic and argumentative assignments. "Reading the Signs" question 2 asks students whether Craig's categories (which he devised in 1990) still apply to advertising today, whereas question 3 has students consider Craig's ethical take on the techniques he describes. To complicate matters, question 4 asks students to study commercials that accompany relatively gender-neutral TV programs for evidence of stereotyped gender portrayal. The most challenging and wide-reaching question is the fifth, which has students enter the debate over the origins of gender identity. For this question, you'll want to read a number of selections that address the social construction of gender roles (see the Introduction to Chapter 7 and the Aaron Devor reading in that chapter), along with Deborah Blum's argument for biological origins (also in Chapter 7).

If you like to include audiovisual material in your course, exposés of the ugly ways women are presented in advertising could add a real edge to your discussions. The *Killing Us Softly* series by Jean Kilbourne started with a now dated but still relevant film of the same name (1979) and adds another dimension to Craig's discussion of gender portrayal in advertising. Addressing the ways women function as signs (of sexuality, passivity, even stupidity) in advertising, these films show many sample ads and deliver lively, accurate interpretations of them. They have never failed to trigger a strong response from our students. The original film has been followed up with three sequels: *Killing Us Softly Again* (1987), *Killing Us Softly 3* (1999), and *Killing Us Softly 4* (2010). It's worth checking to see whether your school's film library has these films, or you can view them online.

JENNIFER L. POZNER

Dove's "Real Beauty" Backlash (p. 194)

Pozner's selection poses a real conundrum: Is the much-ballyhooed Dove "Real Beauty" ad campaign revolutionary in its use of older, non-svelte models, or is it hypocritical in pretending to be trail-blazing while still promoting the usual beauty products to women? There's no easy answer here, and certainly Pozner doesn't think so. Yet what leads her to weigh in on the side of the Dove campaign is the reaction of male media commentators, such as Richard Roeper, who decry the appearance of ordinary women, not the "fantasy babes" (Roeper's words) that they prefer. Expect a strong student reaction that may split along gender lines. We've found that female students—even those who are consumers of fashion magazines and emulate the looks and styles of their favorite models—see nothing wrong with the Dove campaign, and some find it refreshing. Male students tend to have more of a mixed reaction, particularly because Pozner so sharply attacks the male media critics. Although your male students might not go so far as to share one commentator's claim that the Dove models are "frightening," a few may agree with another claim that "ads should be about the beautiful people." You might ask your students about the reaction to the Dove campaign: Why do they think it has triggered such controversy? Why do they think male critics of the campaign even care about ads for women's moisturizers? And you might compare the Dove models with other nontraditional models such as the sixtysomething Cindy Joseph. Why is *she* not considered controversial? (You can find Joseph featured in catalogues such as J. Jill or magazines for middle-aged women such as *More*.) Such questions can lead to a serious discussion of the mythologies surrounding physical appearance for both men and women in our culture. It could also lead to a broader discussion of the role fantasy plays in marketing and advertising. Why do we often assume that models shouldn't be ordinary people? If your students respond that "otherwise no one would buy the product," well, you might note that the Dove ad campaign has been successful, or at least the expanded product line that it promotes has been. And you might tie the Dove campaign to the discussion of fantasy as a marketing strategy in the Introduction to this chapter.

For a creative assignment, try assigning "Reading the Signs" question 1, which has students assume the role of one of the Dove models and write a response to one of the male critics Pozner quotes. We've framed this as a journal topic, but it could work well as an essay prompt, particularly if you want students to develop skills in refuting an argument. Question 2 invites students to support or refute Pozner's conclusion that the backlash to the Real Beauty campaign demonstrates its value in combating gender stereotypes; question 3 asks them to assess the male criticism of these ads. For a broader topic, see question 4, which goes beyond the Dove ads to include similar ones such as Nike's "My Butt Is Big" campaign and asks students to address the conundrum mentioned above: Are such ads revolutionary or just more of the same objectification of women? Question 5 moves to Dove's 2013 "Real Beauty Sketches," an experiment involving a forensic artist's sketches of real women based on their self-descriptions; the goal was to convince women that they are physically more attractive than they assume. At six minutes, the film can easily be viewed in class (visit http://realbeautysketches.dove.us).

GLORIA STEINEM

Sex, Lies, and Advertising (p. 197)

Steinem's essay has been a perennial favorite among *Signs of Life*'s users since the first edition, and as it has become a must-read for any class that addresses either advertising or gender issues. Steinem exposes the compromises magazines — particularly women's magazines — must make when soliciting advertising. Forget about freedom of the press: The advertising industry makes tremendous demands related not only to its ads, as one might expect, but to editorial content as well. And Steinem documents these demands thoroughly. Many of our students have found this essay shocking, claiming their eyes have been opened to a practice they never realized existed. Some, insulted at being conned by advertising disguised as "journalism," have vowed that they'll now think twice about buying popular magazines. If you want your students to cover a fresh topic in your class, assign this reading.

Note that this is an updated version of Steinem's now-classic essay. The major change is a preface, in which Steinem describes the many reactions to the original publication of "Sex, Lies, and Advertising" in *Ms.*, reactions that ranged from bitter sneering to outright celebration. You'll find this preface extremely useful for its creation of an historical context and its documentation of actual readers' responses to a text. Be sure to notice that Steinem dubs as the "most rewarding response" the inclusion of her essay on college reading lists!

We've never had trouble generating lively discussion about the Steinem essay. Her writing is clear, concrete, and accessible, so your students should be able to handle the selection's length. Some students may find the term *complementary copy* puzzling, but you can ask their peers to help explain it. When assigning the essay, you could ask students to look through magazines they have at home to see whether Steinem's argument about complementary copy applies to them ("Reading the Signs" questions 2, 3, and 4 encourage and structure such explorations). Have them look also for instances of favorable product placement and advertorials (another technique some students have trouble identifying). We urge you to ask your students to bring in one of their magazines and present their findings to the class. Be forewarned that some students have trouble distinguishing between copy and advertising. That difficulty actually proves Steinem's point, but it also means that you may need to spend some time covering the difference between the two. We've found that Steinem's claims hold for most magazines — certainly for all women's magazines, but for men's and special interest magazines as well (*Car and Driver*, *Sky and Telescope*, *Log Home Living*, *Cat Fancy* — the list is virtually endless). It is least true for general-interest magazines such as *Time*, but even there you'll see some complementary copy and many advertorials, and students could develop Steinem's discussion of why the content of these magazines seems less influenced by the ad industry. Finally, question 1 asks students to explore the First Amendment implications of Steinem's revelations. We've made it a journal topic, but it could be adapted to a formal essay assignment as well.

JULIETT B. SCHOR

Selling to Children: The Marketing of Cool (p. 218)

Students often assume that they are impervious to advertising, as they cherish a self-perception of being logical, independent thinkers who are immune to being conned. And thus they sometimes dismiss critiques of advertising that skewer the industry as being "much ado about nothing." But Schor's exposé of the techniques marketers use to attract children may give them pause. Beginning with an overview of the history of "cool," the selection first outlines how advertisers adopted edgy street culture as a tool, first to attract teen consumers and then later to nab young children. Students are likely to recognize quickly how "cool" has become a dominant marketing motif; they may be aware that it has infiltrated children's TV programming and games. Push your students beyond whatever nostalgic memories they may have about watching Nickelodeon as a kid, to explore what Schor calls the network's "core philosophy: *kids rule*." In other words, it encourages a dichotomy of (cool) kid versus (boring) adult, in which the "product" becomes a hero in triumph over parents. Is the industry claim that it is simply empowering children credible? What interests stand behind such a claim? Be sure to extend your discussion to some of the larger ramifications of this hard-sell marketing to kids. What are advertisers teaching children about the value of material goods? Do students see any link between such advertising practices and the unquenchable desire for consumer products? What problems, if any, do they see in "kids . . . getting older younger"? Have they witnessed this trend in younger siblings, and if so, what is their response? As Schor points out, the branding of children's products, and the advent of cool as an advertising theme targeted at the young, was well established in the 1990s, and thus today's college-age students were part of that target group. Do your students recall their responses to such pitches? Did their parents impose restrictions on their consuming behavior? What was their attitude toward consumption at the time, and how does it compare to their current attitudes and behavior as consumers?

A logical next step is to ask students to analyze children's advertising based on this selection; accordingly, "Reading the Signs" question 1 asks students to evaluate semiotically an advertisement directed at children. You might suggest they study the advertising that accompanies Saturday cartoon shows, encouraging them to see the relationship between the ads and the shows—often the two are indistinguishable. As is likely to emerge in class discussion, children's advertising, especially in its more manipulative forms, often triggers calls for more regulation to protect these youngest (and most vulnerable) of consumers. Question 2 has the class debate whether such regulation is warranted; we suggest that teams work energetically to amass examples from print and broadcast media and from the Internet and to use them as evidence supporting their position. Implicit in Schor's discussion is an approach to market research that parallels the techniques described by James B. Twitchell in "What We Are to Advertisers." Accordingly, question 3 asks students to assess whether Twitchell's claim that marketing relies on mass stereotypes applies to children or tweens. This question can be challenging because children's advertising often appeals to a sense of individualism — "You're special!" — and students need to be skeptical when such claims go out to millions of kids. Finally, question 4 sends them to Thomas Frank's "Commodify Your Dissent" (Chapter 1) to explore how tween advertising commodifies coolness and edginess.

JOSEPH TUROW

The Daily You: How the New Advertising Industry Is Defining Your Identity and Your Worth (p. 228)

The consumer in you feels like buying a new watch or pair of running shoes or whatever, so you go online to check out the possibilities. Sure enough, after your search, magically you start receiving pop-ads for watches, running shoes, or that whatever. Or is it magic? Not at all, reveals Joseph Turow, in this selection that outlines the motives and means of advertisers' "data mining" of consumers on the Internet. To illustrate how this supposed "personalization" of advertising works, Turow early on narrates the experience of a fictional middle-class family and its discomfort, even "mortification," with being so precisely profiled online. Some of your students may adopt a blasé attitude toward these "tailored commercial messages," claiming that consumers can just ignore them, or, as Turow himself mentions, they may even enjoy receiving custom-made ads. Ask them about the fictional family's responses: Are they overreacting to digital profiling? Is the father's sense that he is being subject to social discrimination valid? Some students may see the Internet as an invaluable source of information; but as Turow points out, digital profiling can actually limit one's opportunities to the identity that marketers have decided we have and thus the information that they have decided we need. Their motives and values are revealed in the connotations of terms they use to describe consumers: "targets" and "waste." Ask your students: Would they feel "creeped out" knowing that they are categorized as "waste"?

This selection is ripe for assignments that address the ethical and social implications of online media profiling. The first "Reading the Signs" question invites students to write a letter to the fictional couple Turow describes, advising them on how to avoid digital surveillance; for inspiration, students might consult Gloria Steinem's call for action at the end of "Sex, Lies, and Advertising" in this chapter. Question 2 prompts an in-class debate on whether online profiling of consumers is problematic; this debate could serve as collective brainstorming for students' individual essays on the topic. Turow suggests that although corporations such as Google profit hugely from collecting consumers' personal information, the consumer does not reap such benefits. Accordingly, question 3 asks students to argue whether such corporations should compensate Internet users for their data. For a semiotic analysis, question 4 has students examine the Web site of one of the data-tracking companies that Turow mentions (or one of the many clones that have sprung up since he wrote his essay). In doing so, students should heed our advice throughout the book: Don't take things at face value. The most challenging question, the fifth, asks students to respond to Turow's call for a "serious discussion" of how social profiling constitutes a hidden, and thus insidious, form of social discrimination. To broaden students' thinking about this topic, you might have them consult Gloria Steinem's "Sex, Lies, and Advertising" and Stephanie Clifford and Quentin Hardy's "Attention, Shoppers: Store Is Tracking Your Cell" in Chapter 1.

JULIA B. CORBETT

A Faint Green Sell: Advertising and the Natural World (p. 235)

One of the central moves in semiotic analysis is exploring the social values and mythologies underlying a sign, and Julia B. Corbett takes this strategy to heart in her thorough study of advertising's exploitation of environmentalism in order to peddle their wares. One of the longer pieces in *Signs of Life*, "A Faint Green Sell" offers a comprehensive discussion of the various ways that advertising, which Corbett terms a fundamentally "brown" business, invokes environmental values and natural imagery. Corbett's ideas are accessible, but because her essay is fairly complex, you might ask students to outline it or write their own summaries of her six main arguments about green advertising. The effort will be well worth it, as Corbett moves from the history of advertising and the mass media to explore specific uses of nature in ads, from the portrayal of animals to the use of "nature as backdrop." Given Corbett's precise categorization of green ad techniques, a productive class activity would be to ask students, either individually or in groups, to engage in hands-on analysis of ads, both print and video. Thanks to the proliferation of more environmentally friendly products, you and your class should have no trouble finding such ads in magazines and on YouTube, but be sure that students don't simply study ads for the Prius or Seventh Generation detergent. Encourage them to consider how ordinary products are wrapped in a green mantle, even though they may be as toxic as an electronics waste dump, and how eco-unfriendly businesses like oil companies present themselves as if they were blessed by John Muir himself. This activity will enable the class to have a deeper understanding of what Corbett's title refers to and will prepare them well for writing their own essays on green advertising.

This selection lends itself to a wide variety of assignments, from textual analysis to philosophical contemplation. "Reading the Signs" question 1 starts by asking students to contemplate whether advertising can in fact really be green. Here you might ask students to consider the link between advertising and consumption, particularly consumption of mass-produced, throwaway convenience items. James Robert's "The Treadmill of Consumption" (Chapter 1) provides a complementary argument that could help students develop their ideas. Question 2 has students focus on one category of green ads that Corbett discusses, those that use nature as a sublime backdrop; as we suggest, travel magazines are a good source of such ads (and the editorial content tends to duplicate that same pattern). For a focused textual analysis, assign question 3, which has students use Corbett's selection as a critical framework to analyze a single ad; you could complicate this question by asking students to interpret several ads or a full ad campaign for a product. For a variant, question 6 asks students to look at the ways ads for decidedly anti-green corporations use natural imagery (ads for Chevron and Monsanto are particularly good choices). If you want your class to address the values and ideologies that underlie green advertising, assign question 4, which asks them to apply Laurence Shames's concept of Americans' "hunger for more" to green advertising, or question 5, which focuses on the fundamental opposition between advertising and environmental values. We framed this as a class debate, but it makes a challenging essay prompt as well.

Portfolio of Advertisements (color insert)

We feel that it is essential to include some ads that your entire class could share. You'll find that the ads are ideal for semiotic readings as well as for discussion of audience, purpose, and style. They also relate to some of the broader themes, such as gender, that emerge throughout *Signs of Life*. You can use the portfolio in a number of ways. It's perfect for class discussion because every student will have the ads in his or her text and can refer easily to details. Several of the ads work well studied along with one or more of the readings in the text. A discussion of the Buffalo Exchange jeans ad, for instance, could be enhanced by referring to Thomas Frank's selection in Chapter 1 or Steve Craig's in Chapter 2. The Frank essay can come in handy as well when analyzing the Sanuk Yoga Mat Sandals; that ad's nostalgia appeal calls for a careful identification and semiotic reading of the ad's details (you could also bring to your students' attention the way the ad echoes Robert Indiana's iconic "love" poster from the 1960s). In class, you might create small groups and have each interpret an ad of its members' own choosing; then the class could vote on the ads they consider most and least effective and discuss the significance of the results. If students find any of the ads problematic, ask them what alternative appeals they'd suggest. How would they redesign the ads?

Chapter 3
VIDEO DREAMS
Television and Cultural Forms

Your students will be the experts when you cover this chapter, for many of them are TV junkies, proudly asserting that they've watched every episode of *The Big Bang Theory* or *Game of Thrones* or (fill in the blank). While not all students are so glued to the tube, many are (or were, in their early teen years), and they may be far more familiar with current TV programs than you are. Take advantage of their expertise by asking them to shape your class discussion. Your students are likely to know which current shows are the best ones to consider in light of Neal Gabler's essay about the ubiquity of "friends" on television, for instance, or they can tell you whether Lena Dunham's character in *Girls* continues to engage in humiliating rendezvous with men. Your job will be to steer them toward writing careful critical analyses of the shows they enjoy and often identify with, and they can resist critical discussion of them because they may feel their own tastes are under attack. (The "Exploring the Signs of Television" box question, accordingly, allows students to explore their TV viewing habits and how they have changed over time.) Be sure your students understand that asking *why* this image or this story appears in a video or TV program is not the same as evaluating their personal worth as individuals. Indeed, you should expect the anti-analysis argument that protests, "It's just entertainment." You might respond with the central semiotic insight that nothing is innocent. In fact, media products are designed precisely to appeal to a culture's dreams and desires—that's what makes them entertaining—and what you're doing is studying the nature and social significance of such appeals. You could study some of the images included in the chapter—an ad for *The Walking Dead* (p. 257), for example—and ask them how, in different ways, they are constructed to appeal to their audience. Are they really "*just* entertainment"? If any students think so, they are more likely to feel that way about *The Simpsons*; you may need to remind them that the cartoon's originator, Matt Groening, began it as a self-conscious skewering of mainstream American culture. The "Discussing the Signs of Television" question is further intended to nurture such a critical approach by asking students to go beyond a show's surface appeal to ask, "What is the program really saying?" The "Reading about TV and Community Online" question has a similar goal. By asking students to explore what viewer forums for TV programs reveal about their interests and cultural tastes, we hope that they will analyze how TV shows shape a common identity for their fans. Indeed, they work to create a community that, in some ways, serves as a potent form of promotion, even if viewers do not intend their participation to serve that purpose.

To facilitate class discussion, you'll want to ensure that students all have seen the same videos or programs. Thanks to the Internet, you could watch them on Hulu.com, on a show's own Web site, or on YouTube. We recommend that you record videos or TV programs and view them in class before analyzing them; that way, you can stop and study details or go back and watch significant scenes a second time. Students won't always remember details, or the details they recall won't necessarily be the most significant ones. Don't worry about using all your class time. You could focus on particular scenes in long shows, and single segments of TV programs usually provide plenty to analyze (a half-hour show typically translates into about 22 minutes, sans commercials). You should feel free to zap those commercials—unless, of course, you want to study what products are pitched to which audiences and how those products relate to the programs they sponsor.

The chapter begins with Nick Serpe engaging in a serious contemplation of the political implications of RTV; if you use this selection, keep in mind that reality TV has been around for two decades now, and it may seem like "normal" programming to students who have been exposed to little else. The next two selections each offer comprehensive cultural interpretations of a single show focused on Southern women (*Nashville* and *Here Comes Honey Boo-Boo*) and are ideal if you are emphasizing either a semiotic approach or gender as a theme. The next pair of readings focuses on edgy TV, with Carl Matheson exploring the self-conscious irony of *The Simpsons* and Natasha Simons focusing on the decidedly problematic heroes in *Mad Men*. Jane Hu's reading of *Girls* follows, focusing on the intersection of sex, eating, class, and sex, while Willa Paskin's essay on *Devious Maids* examines the show through the lens of class consciousness. Neal Gabler closes the chapter with a study of the plethora of TV chums and pals, locating the fad of faux friendship a reflection of Americans' feelings of solitude and isolation that TV ironically has helped to produce.

NICK SERPE

Reality Pawns: The New Money TV (p. 268)

The Great Recession ushered in many changes in Americans' lives, from the need to brew their own Joe rather than indulging in a Starbucks' latte to living back home with mom and dad after graduating college. It's no surprise that TV — especially reality TV — has exploited the ongoing shifts in the American economy, turning financial travail into, well, entertainment. In this indictment of shows like *Repo* and *Pawn Stars*, Serpe suggests that viewers' attraction to them is based on an extreme free-market mentality that delights in an economic battle in which the winners trick the "losers" and successfully grab their cars, houses, family treasures—a perfect survival-of-the-fittest plot line. The appeal of such fare depends, in part, on voyeurism and a delight in watching contestants lose and get conned. You could connect this discussion with that in the Introduction to this chapter, in which we talk about how *schadenfreude* underlies so many reality TV programs. It's likely that your students will accept this explanation, although be prepared for some to dismiss it by saying "Oh, RTV is just fun to watch" or "It's only a TV show." If you get that response, push them harder: *Why* is it amusing to watch pawnbrokers give customers less than their artifacts are worth? Or a repo man slip away with a single mom's only source of transportation? If you can stand doing so, have the class watch a clip of one of these programs. How do students respond? Do they consider the program entertaining? Why or why not?

We think it's important that students understand the values inherent in reality TV, or else they will have trouble grasping the second part of Serpe's argument. Focus their attention particularly on his description of the "common tropes" that characterize these shows, tropes suggesting a dog-eat-dog ethos that, as Serpe puts it, creates "nostalgia for simpler capitalism." If students balk at the political angle, encourage them to look beyond their own beliefs and to consider some political controversies, such as the debate over Social Security. Traditionally, of course, Social Security was instituted as a retirement plan to which everyone contributed and from which all could benefit. With the Tea Party attacks on so-called "entitlements," that sense of "social" security changes. If your students don't see a connection, have them consider Rick Harrison's call to "reeducate everyone." That comment alone should give anyone pause.

This selection can prompt a range of meaty assignments, especially argumentative topics. The simplest is "Reading the Signs" question 1, which has students assess Serpe's tone in this essay. For an analytic question, assign number 2, which calls for a focused reading of one of the programs that Serpe discusses. Question 3 invites students to respond to Serpe's broader claims about the links between right-wing politics and debt-and-credit RTV programs. For a topic that requires students to do some outside work, try question 4, which has them research the TV show *Queen for a Day* (1956–1964) and to compare it to the "busted-economy" shows that Serpe discusses. Another comparison prompt, question 5 sends students to Jon Mooallem's "The Self-Storage Self" in Chapter 1 to examine the lives of RTV characters through the lens of real-life self-storage users. Just who are the reality pawns?

CLAIRE MIYE STANFORD

You've Got the Wrong Song: Nashville *and Country Music Feminism (p. 276)*

If you were to look up *oxymoron* in a dictionary, you might expect to find the phrase "country music feminism" as an example. After all, between Tammy Wynette's 1968 hit tune "Stand By Your Man" and the current popularity of "Bro-country" ballads, feminism is not the sort of thing that one would associate with country music today. And yet, just as there is a feminist response to hip-hop machismo, so too is there a tradition of country music stars (like Dolly Parton) who are no mere Tammy Wynette pushovers, and in this analysis of the television series *Nashville*, Claire Miye Stanford explores the ways in which country music can indeed express a woman's voice.

Stanford's selection, while nonacademic in style (it was first published in the *Los Angeles Review of Books*), is richly nuanced in its analysis. Stanford complicates the usual notion of "female-driven" television by analyzing Nashville's skewing of so many conventions, from the role of southern women, to TV genres (is this a soap opera or workplace drama?). Your students have lots to consider given Stanford's superbly succinct historical range in this selection. Even before you discuss the essay (and maybe in a session before you plan to do so), consider using "Reading the Signs" question 1, which asks students to explain what the term *feminism* connotes. We suggest this as an in-class exercise, but you can adapt it as a reading log entry. However you pose the question, it will reveal to you a lot about your students' assumptions and how they might respond to Stanford's essay.

This selection is ideal for triggering insightful analytic assignments, as Stanford poses lots of questions, and answers, that provide a strong critical framework. "Reading the Signs" question 2 is the most basic, as it asks students to assess Stanford's claim about *Nashville* (you also could extend the question to another woman-centered program, such as *Orange is the New Black*). Similarly, question 3 turns the focus to female country music artists, while question 4 shifts it to different musical genre, focusing on Lady Gaga (again, let students substitute newer artists). For a link with gender and regional concerns, question 5 sends students to Michelle Dean's selection on *Honey Boo Boo*. Does that show have the "wrong" song? Challenge your students to decide.

MICHELLE DEAN

Here Comes the Hillbilly, Again (p. 283)

Okay. We bet a lot of you sneer at *Honey Boo Boo*. Maybe some of you don't. But whatever gut responses are, shut them off until you read Michelle Dean's insightful look at a huge section of American culture: the inheritors of what was formerly called "hillbilly" culture, now extended to middle-class white Americans who are not part of the blue state mood. The Tea Party's expansive influence on our country's political system is enough to let you know why we say that this demographic is "huge." We include this reading for a number of reasons: not simply because we should not ignore a pop cultural phenomenon that galvanizes many Americans (who might include your students); but also that given the focus of *Signs of Life*, Dean's discussion of *Honey Boo Boo* more pointedly locates it in a segment of American ideology, and thus this reading is exactly the sort of analytic wake-up call that semiotics can deliver.

Depending on your school's demographic make-up, you might approach this selection variously. If you teach in the South, don't predict your students' evaluations of the program to be positive or negative, but some of the show's details might resonate with them more than to Northeastern hipsters. For both groups of students, Dean's brief history of the term "hillbilly" can prove instructive. Indeed, before you even assign this reading, you might ask the class to do a quick freewrite on what the term means to them. Then, as you discuss Dean's article, tease out the racial implications of the hillbilly stereotypes that she mentions: Why might they appeal to the show's fans? Why might poor white Southerners feel either attracted or repelled by the signs attached to stereotypical hillbillies?

Dean's essay is great for assignments that focus narrowly on a program or that address cultural and class issues more broadly. For a focused prompt, use "Reading the Signs" question 1, which asks students to address Dean's assumption that a show like *Honey Boo Boo* exploits the lower edge of white American culture for the sake of entertainment. If you wish to complicate the question, you could ask students to compare *HBB* with an older program that focuses on the characters of a similar demographic, such as *The Beverly Hillbillies*. For comparative assignments, consider question 2, which sends students to Nick Serpe's selection in this chapter on reality TV programs that exploit the plight of those suffering from the Great Recession, and question 3, which invites students to explore Dean's link between *HBB* and a program like *Jersey Shore* (not hillbilly, but also decidedly not upper-crust). If your course theme focuses on advertising, your students might enjoy question 4, which asks them to analyze vintage and current ads for that "hillbilly" drink, Mountain Dew. Of course, your students can now substitute scads of alternatives for that corporate mainstay.

CARL MATHESON

The Simpsons, *Hyper-Irony, and the Meaning of Life (p. 287)*

Since 1989, *The Simpsons* has been an American pop culture institution and may well be one of your students' (and perhaps your own) favorite TV programs. This alone may make the *The Simpsons* a challenge to analyze because it is often difficult to be objective about things that you really like. But *The Simpsons* is challenging for a second reason; given its self-appointed role as America's most popular satirizer of American pop culture, the show (like its grittier counterpart, *South Park*) may seem to be above critique. But don't let that fool you: *The Simpsons* is as much a reflection of contemporary American society as it is a parody of it, and it shares many traits with the culture that it lampoons.

To explain the contradiction: While *The Simpsons* delights in skewering American hypercapitalism and consumerism, it is itself a gigantic commercial enterprise, with high rent advertising rates and every kind of commodity spin-off, from dolls to watch faces. Its success means that it draws in millions of viewers, exposing them to the ads its sponsors run, at top dollar per spot, even as it massages their egos by assuring them of their immunity to commercialism. Keep that in mind when a student insists that the show is a devastating critique of consumerism.

Note as well how the "star" of *The Simpsons* has changed over the years. In the beginning, witty and wicked Bart Simpson, whose sharp tongue added phrases to the language even as he ridiculed much that is ridiculous in American society, held center stage. But for a number of years, Bart has played second fiddle to Homer, a dopey buffoon who specializes in low comedy. Don't be fooled here by any particular plot line that Homer may be involved in, because the real significance isn't in the plot, it's in the antics. *The Simpsons* plots tend to be thrown together loosely to create a stage for the gags. The show may act as if it is sending a social message of some sort, but the real significance lies in the rapid pace of punch lines and dopey situations, situations that Homer specializes in creating.

This shift from Bart to Homer parallels a related shift in American entertainment from sophisticated to adolescent humor. Consider *Malcolm in the Middle*, which at first featured its title character's high IQ but then relegated that detail to a sideshow as Malcolm's antics become just as stupid as his cretinous brothers' and parents'. Or consider *Family Guy* and its flatulent humor or *Jackass* and its legacy. Increasingly, American entertainment, especially humor, is conforming to the crude but edgy sensibility of male adolescents, reflecting the culture industry's decision to abandon past standards of taste and restraint in the name of profits. This relaxation of standards itself reflects a general trend within American social codes of behavior in which adolescent conduct is rapidly becoming a norm. If your students object, ask them if they have been "flipped off" recently (or have themselves flipped someone else off) for the least social offense. What sorts of language — that is, potty language — are they accustomed to hearing and using? How do people address each other in reader's comments on online news sites, even such mainstream ones like *The Los Angeles Times*? (Answer: with vulgar flames.) To point this out is not necessarily to criticize anyone, but simply to draw attention to the essentially immature behavior of Americans these days, a code that is reflected in what entertains us.

You'll probably have students divided in assessing *The Simpsons* and Matheson's analysis of it. "Reading the Signs" questions 1 and 3 thus invite students to support or refute two of Matheson's points about the program, while Question 2 has them extend his concept of hyper-irony to other media examples. We've included two comparison questions: Question 4 prompts students to compare the show with its Web site (which we find even more fully commercialized), and question 5 has them compare it with another comic program such as *Family Guy*.

NATASHA SIMONS

Mad Men *and the Paradox of the Past (p. 300)*

Simons's selection is a perfect illustration of advice you are likely to be giving your students: In writing a cultural analysis, they shouldn't assume there is a "right" or a "wrong" answer to your assignments; rather, they should aim for strong logic and specific evidence to persuade their readers of the validity and superiority of their thesis. In her consideration of *Mad Men*, Simons observes that liberal and conservative viewers typically have diametrically opposed takes on this retro 1950s program. Liberals tend to interpret the show's overt sexism and racism as proof of the triumph of progressive thinking, Simons claims, while conservatives may wax nostalgic at the pre-1960s traditionalism and unquestioned values. Similarly, in our own conversations with others, we've heard debates about whether the show should be read ironically or at face value. It is precisely because *Mad Men* seems so fluid and invites such a range of responses that it challenges students' argumentative and rhetorical abilities. "Reading the Signs" question 1 asks students to probe claims about the conservative–liberal split by interviewing viewers of both political tendencies about their response to the program. They should use their results as evidence for their evaluation of Simons' thesis. Question 2 similarly asks students to address the audience's mixed response, but this time we intend for them to use as evidence their own analysis of the show and its characters. *Mad Men* seems like a hyperrealistic depiction of 1950s business culture, but of course, with the exception of the occasional returning student, our students have no direct knowledge of that time period. We thus designed question 3, which has students read either Sloan Wilson's fictional *The Man in the Grey Flannel Suit* or Vance Packard's exposé *The Hidden Persuaders* for help in determining the show's level of realism. If you are emphasizing semiotics, you will find that the show lends itself well to this approach and will want to assign question 4, which calls for a semiotic reading of a single episode. For a gender focus, question 5 sends students to Aaron Devor's "Gender Role Behaviors and Attitudes" in Chapter 7 for a critical framework to analyze *Man Men*'s in-your-face sexism.

JANE HU

Reality Hunger: On Lena Dunham's* Girls *(p. 304)

Girls is a great topic if you want to explore the complexities of feminist analysis with your students. Like *Sex and the City* before it (an iconic program to which Lena Dunham pays explicit homage), *Girls* features four independent young women trying to make their ways professionally and romantically in New York City. But the often abject nature of their relationships with the men in their lives, along with the propensity of Dunham's character to "get naked," sets up a classic confrontation between Second and Third Wave feminism. Thus a good way to begin a discussion of *Girls* is to explore the differences between a Second Wave feminist analysis of the show, which would condemn the sexual exploitation and objectification of the program's lead characters, and a Third Wave feminist perspective that might highlight the show's sexual realism and the ways in which the women control their own sexuality.

Of course, there is a lot more to *Girls* than sex. The social class status of the main characters is something that your students may not initially recognize: fundamentally upper middle class, the show's protagonists hail from, or attend, expensive and relatively exclusive private colleges, and their world views generally are those of the upper middle class. A good topic for discussion would explore the political significance of the fact that this small slice of American demography is so often taken by television critics as representative of an entire generation of millennials—a generation in which white upper-middle-class young women are a minority, not a typical sample. "Reading the Signs" question 2 challenges students to assess exactly this presupposition of the program: Do the characters realistically portray the lives of millennials? If you're game, we suggest that you ask students to conduct interviews or surveys to create a bank of inductive evidence. And, for a question about the show's class consciousness (or lack thereof), question 6 sends students to Michael Parenti's "Class and Virtue" (in Chapter 4) for help in exploring the often ignored classism underlying the show.

For her part, Jane Hu takes a somewhat formalistic approach to *Girls*, focusing especially on the significant role food plays in the show. Hu's analysis offers a good opportunity to explain the difference between a formalistic and a cultural analysis of a popular cultural artifact. Guiding your students carefully through the ways in which Hu follows a culinary thread through the text of *Girls* can help them understand how formal symbolism can work in a mass media phenomenon, just as in a literary text. Students who are intrigued by Hu's quotidian focus on food might enjoy "Reading the Signs" question 1, which invites a semiotic analysis comparing the lifestyle details represented in *Girls* and the older *Friends* (you could substitute another twentysomething program for the latter if you prefer). Given that sex obviously is a major theme in *Girls*, questions 3 and 4 call for argumentative analyses of the program's depiction of young women's sexuality and intimate behavior. For a somewhat different take on the show, question 5 asks students to assess *Girls*' s possible categorization as "performance art," a prompt ideal for sending students to research what performance art is in the first place.

WILLA PASKIN

Devious Maids *Skewers the One Percent (p. 312)*

If your course centers on the familiar triad of race, class, and gender, this selection is for you. While Paskin does find some flaws in *Devious Maids*, she clearly enjoys the show's depiction of Latina maids who ultimately are cannier and more compassionate than their wealthy white employers. For a focus on race, ask your students to study in particular the depiction of the maids and their bosses. To what extent are they both stereotypical? Is it a breakthrough that the program locates the maids in a moral position that their white bosses never seem to know about, much less occupy? No easy answers here, but challenge your students to construct a solid argument. "Reading the Signs" question 3 asks students to use Michael Omi's categories of racial stereotyping ("In Living Color," Chapter 7) as a critical framework to plumb the racial representations in the show.

You could also ask your class about the representation of women in this program. To what extent are the roles of the selfless domestic and the bitchy boss two extreme characterizations of female identity? And as for the depiction of class, *Devious Maids* once again seems to have it both ways. The one percent are clearly the "baddies" as people, but what about their lifestyle? Is it excoriated the same way as the characters are, or does it remain beyond the pale of criticism, as Paskin herself suggests? Question 1 sends students to Michael Parenti's "Class and Virtue" in Chapter 4 for help in assessing the show's message about class difference, while question 4 asks the class to relate the show's popularity to the current class divisions in America. For a topic that enables your students to contemplate the entire triad, consider assigning number 2, which asks students to compare *Devious Maids* with an earlier program focused on a Latina protagonist, *Ugly Betty* (visit Hulu.com or YouTube for episodes). What differences do students see (if any) in the depiction of the main characters in each program? Are the racial and class tensions more or less pronounced? Or just different? What explanations do students have for their observations?

NEAL GABLER

The Social Networks (p. 315)

We were delighted when we first came upon Neal Gabler's essay on the proliferation of happy friends and family on TV; as Gabler puts it, "the basic unit of television is the flock." We've been long irritated by the unrealistic portrayal of characters always having lots of buddies and pals, ready for a cheery visit 24/7, never alone, always socializing, always partying, always there for an intimate heart-to-heart. "What's wrong with that?" students might ask. "Isn't it better for people to be social than anti-social?" A fair enough question. The history of TV includes very few programs that show people alone. You might come up with a few more, but we think only of the late 1980s *The Days and Nights of Molly Dodd*, a critically acclaimed program that used a single-camera technique that accentuated the protagonist's isolation. It survived for two seasons on NBC, was shown in run-runs on cable, and that was about it. Even Gabler admits that he feels "a little churlish pointing out how phony" TV friendships are. But he also raises a formidable defense of his critique: the crowds of friends and relative are becoming ever-more popular at a time when, in real life, Americans are increasingly isolated and disconnected from each other. Indeed, television itself plays a role in people's alienation as the hours we spend watching the screen mean that we are not spending them in any meaningful human interaction. And, as Gabler also points out, traditional friendship is becoming bastardized when "friending" others on social networking sites becomes a competitive game of seeing who can add up more names than anyone else. If you detect a much-ado-about-nothing response in your class, challenge your students to consider the rather profound implications for human relationships and intimacy that Gabler suggests.

You'll find that Gabler's essay lends itself to both semiotic and more philosophical essay assignments. "Reading the Signs" question 1 invites students to argue for or against the validity of Gabler's central thesis. For this topic, consider asking your students to conduct an interview to gain a sense of why people watch television and the relative importance TV has in their lives, especially compared with interacting with others. For a semiotic topic, try question 2, which asks students to analyze the significance of friendship in an episode of a friend-heavy program. To extend the issues to social networking sites, question 3 has students to take on Gabler's contention that Facebook offers "friendship lite." Students can refine their argument if you also ask them to read "Students Addicted to Social Media" in Chapter 5. For an updated analysis of TV friendships, question 4 sends students to Jane Hu's essay on *Girls*, a show that superficially resembles some of the programs Gabler describes but that also comes with a slew of decidedly uncomfortable relationships.

Chapter 4

THE HOLLYWOOD SIGN

The Culture of American Film

It's not surprising that writing instructors have long used films as texts for student analysis, because the best films can offer the complexity, narrative structures, characters, and symbol systems of a novel or story. Film has also been a favorite subject of semiotic analysis, and with good reason. Movies are rich sign systems, deliberately designed to appeal to an audience's values and desires, both reflecting and shaping a society's dreams. We find that a semiotic approach can help students make the leap from writing simply about their judgments of movies — why they like a particular film — to writing critical analyses of them. Because movies are so much a part of their lives, it's sometimes difficult for students to interpret them critically. They may say, "But it's just entertaining!" Your answer? "Of course it's entertaining. But why does *this* movie make you laugh? Or cry? *How* did the movie trigger a particular response in you?" This chapter is designed precisely to help students move from an audience-appreciation response to a critical response. Accordingly, the "Exploring the Signs of Film" question asks students to examine their favorite films, reflecting on what their personal preferences reveal about their own tastes, values, and beliefs. In essence, students will explore how their cinematic tastes serve as signs of their individual identity. The "Discussing the Signs of Film" question looks at film as a broader social phenomenon, this time asking students to consider why blockbuster hits achieve such a status. For this question, have your class identify the most recent mega-hits, locate the films in the context of other popular fads, and consider the social values and ideologies that the films manipulate. We think students should realize how Hollywood's image-making machine works its magic on its own products, so the "Reading Film Online" exercise invites students to study the Web site of a recent film or the posters that advertise films. Students should consider this question: How does the packaging of a film affect a viewer's understanding of its meaning?

As with Chapter 3 on television, it's useful to structure class discussion around a common visual text; but given time constraints, you may be unable to watch an entire feature film in class. Some movies are ninety minutes long, so if your class runs in a two-hour block you probably can watch one movie in class. If that's not an option, assign a current film for homework (students should be able to rent it online or legally download it), or check to see if your campus has a film library where you can put a movie on reserve. Your students are likely to possess a tremendously high level of cinematic literacy — so high that it may pose a problem. When discussing a movie, you may need to steer students away from celebrity worship, chitchat about what film a particular actor has appeared in recently, or another actor's recent DUI arrest. At times, you just have to say that celebrity gossip isn't the same as a critical discussion. You may also have to remind students that a public relations spin on a movie isn't the same as an objective analysis of it. Just because Madonna said she was "telling all" in *Truth or Dare* (1991), for example, doesn't mean that's the case. You'll be able to keep students on track if you remind them of that semiotic question "Why?" Keep at them to ask: "Why this plot twist?" Or "Why a male rather than a female character?" Or "Why a black actor for this role?" When you do this, they will be on their way to writing sharp analytic papers.

Because the readings in the chapter address various myths that influence films, you'll find the chapter easy to adapt to your course's focus and your students' interests. Linda Seger begins the chapter by outlining the "universal" story lines that give shape to the mythologies underlying many popular films. The chapter then moves to a trio of readings that address cultural and ethnic stereotypes in film. A paired set, the next two articles shed light on Hollywood's historically skewed representation of women: Jessica Hagedorn's selection on Asian women in film and Helena Andrews's comparison of the gender representations in two roughly thematically related films, *The Butler* and *The Help*. Filling out the trio, Matt Zoller Seitz reveals the ideology underlying the "magical Negro" character. Films are, of course, ultimately a highly conventionalized medium and thus are ripe for semiotic analyses; the next two selections are ideal for a class that highlights the semiotic approach with a focused subject in mind. Michael Parenti examines social class, and David Denby analyzes the stock characters in teen movies. Concluding the chapter are two selections that offer a broader cultural analysis: Michael Agresta explores how the fate of the cinematic Western has floundered thanks to changing attitudes toward American history; then Christine Folch provides a full cultural explanation for why Americans flock to fantasy in their films, while the Indian fans of Bollywood flicks couldn't care less for this genre.

LINDA SEGER

Creating the Myth (p. 334)

Linda Seger's clear, accessible introduction to cultural myths that dominates film is our lead article, as it provides a tidy critical framework for analyzing a broad range of films. Its central argument — that successful films employ archetypes that tap into universal human desires — is sensible but still open to debate and modification. This essay complements Robert B. Ray's "The Thematic Paradigm" (Chapter 6) in that Seger focuses on heroic myths, but unlike Ray, she traces classic hero patterns through a single film, *Star Wars*. She also complicates the heroic myth by examining what she calls "broken" characters and combination myths; this examination will give you great flexibility in class discussion, as most films fit her scheme somehow. Seger also raises some interesting open-ended questions (for instance, why the *Rambo* films were so successful). Herself a screenwriter, Seger wrote this selection for a readership of aspiring screenwriters, and that shapes her tone and attitudes. Her status as an industry insider helps to explain her apparent endorsement of using existing myths in film — she doesn't recommend originality in screenplays. You may want to discuss that essentially conservative viewpoint with your students, who might naïvely assume that imagination counts for something in Hollywood ("Reading the Signs" question 1 addresses this issue).

If you're covering both the Ray and Seger selections, consider assigning question 2, which calls for a gender-based comparison of the two approaches to heroes. Question 3 sends students to Michael Parenti's essay for help in analyzing *Pretty Woman* and *Juno*, while question 4 asks them to examine the archetype-rich *Titanic* or a segment of *The Lord of the Rings*. For a possible research topic, consider assigning question 5, which solicits an evaluation of Seger's suggestion that screenwriters use the archetype-filled Grimm's fairy tales for inspiration. A successful essay in response to this prompt would show a thorough and accurate reading of several such tales. Perhaps the most challenging question is the last, which asks students to explore the character types in *The Hunger Games* (you could easily substitute any mainstream film). We call this prompt "challenging" because many students identify closely with the Hunger Games trilogy, and they will need to set aside their adolescent experience as fans of these films and instead put on an objective analytic hat.

JESSICA HAGEDORN

Asian Women in Film: No Joy, No Luck (p. 343)

Jessica Hagedorn's selection is great for courses that focus on either gender or ethnicity. While you're not likely to be surprised by her argument—films tend to relegate Asian women to the traditional whore/angel dichotomy—your students may not have considered this pattern at all. Ask them to interpret the photos of Michelle Yeoh (p. 346) and Anna May Wong (p. 346): To what extent do these actresses illustrate Hagedorn's point? (Yeoh is best known as Jackie Chan's costar in *Supercop*, and in this photo she plays a Chinese secret agent in *Tomorrow Never Dies*; Wong was an early twentieth-century actress who appeared in *The Thief of Baghdad* [1924] and played a prostitute in *Shanghai Express* [1932].) We should warn you that students might be unhappy with Hagedorn's criticism of *The Joy Luck Club*, a film that is a sentimental favorite among many students, both male and female and of all ethnic backgrounds. Since many students have seen this film, you might want to combine your discussion of this essay with a viewing of the film to allow your students to test Hagedorn's thesis (see "Reading the Signs" question 1). In one successful class on this essay that we observed, the instructor began by asking students to summarize the stereotypes of Asians, both positive and negative and both from their own experience and from Hagedorn's article, and listing them on the board. The class then watched *The Joy Luck Club*'s opening party scene (about 15 minutes); afterward, a rich discussion ensued about the ways in which the scene reproduced or challenged those stereotypes. This careful, methodical discussion set the stage for students' own analysis of racial representations in film. Of course, students could analyze any film (or TV program) with Asian characters; question 5 invites them to consider racial representations in the popular *Harold and Kumar Go to White Castle*. The challenge for students will be responding to the film analytically, not simply to its stoner humor.

A basic analysis assignment would ask students to view one of the films that Hagedorn mentions (or any other with Asian characters) and interpret its depiction of women. Question 4 is similar, but it has students focus on one of the gender-bending films, such as *M. Butterfly*, that Hagedorn mentions (note that some students may feel uncomfortable watching this film). You can broaden the issues that Hagedorn raises by addressing more generally Hollywood's tendency to stereotype different ethnicities. Question 2 invites the class to stage a debate on this issue; students could prepare for the debate by reading Michael Omi's essay in Chapter 7. These issues apply to other media as well; question 3 invites students to analyze a magazine that targets Asian American readers. As a prewriting exercise, consider bringing to class some such magazines for small groups to study.

HELENA ANDREWS

The Butler *versus* The Help*: Gender Matters (p. 352)*

This selection is ripe for assignments focusing on ethnicity and racial identity, class differences, and even the influence of popular culture. Andrews opens with a question about the stark difference in critical response to *The Help* and *The Butler*, both of which feature African American actors in roles as domestic servants. Why was the former film lambasted for replicating stereotypical images of black women as maids, while the latter was praised for its creation of a "subversive" black character who undermines white privilege? This is a great question, we think, and students will have a lot to consider in evaluating Andrews's own position on the matter. She posits gender difference as the main cause: maids are involved in "women's work" and caring for children, whereas a butler is, well, a manservant, someone who is at least granted privy to a realm of power and authority that remains off-limits to maids. "Reading the Signs" question 1 asks students to study reviews of both films for an essay in which they assess the persuasiveness of Andrews's position. As an alternate, students might conduct the same sort of research and analysis on another film that centers on African American characters; *Twelve Years a Slave*, which Andrews mentions, seems a particularly rich choice. Beyond the racial depictions in a single film, Andrews raises a broader question about whether black actors and producers should even consider portraying a black character in a stereotypical role (even if that role has a basis in history, as with maids and butlers). Question 2 sends students to Michael Omi (Chapter 7) and Matt Zoller Seitz (the next reading) for help in teasing out an answer to this thorny question. In addition to race and gender, Andrews posits class differences as yet another reason the two films garnered such contradictory responses: the butler, Cecil Gaines, worked for no less than the president of the United States, where the maids were employed by a variety of well-to-do Southern families, but none close to reaching the stature of Gaines's boss. Michael Parenti's "Class and Virtue" can help students determine whether class indeed shaped viewers' responses to these films.

MATT ZOLLER SEITZ

The Offensive Movie Cliché That Won't Die (p. 356)

Can there be anything wrong with a film featuring a mild-mannered African American character who, behind the scenes, manages to save the day? Most definitely yes, claims Matt Zoller Seitz in this somewhat strident condemnation of the sugarcoated depiction of African Americans in movies such as *Legendary*. It's not that Seitz objects to a black character being benevolent or insightful or heroic. The problem, he would say, lies in the fact that these characters play second fiddle to a central white protagonist and thus become more like stage props than fully realized people with lives and souls of their own. You should easily get a lively discussion going in response to Seitz's argument. First, some students may have reservations because they find these characters warm and even inspirational. There's nothing wrong with a student feeling inspired by a movie, but such objections can give you an opening for a serious discussion of how signs work in our culture, of what happens when fiction is taken as reality. Further, some students might have strong objections to Seitz's use of the term "magical Negro." They may feel uncomfortable with this term—the common use of "Negro" ended long before they were born—and may want to see it as snide or, worse, racist. But Seitz anticipates that response in his readers not only by giving a brief overview of the history of the word but also by outlining the archetype's history. The character dates from over a hundred years ago with figures such as Uncle Remus, Seitz explains, and continues to Spike Lee's popularizing it in 2001 after a spate of films that included African American sidekicks who served to support white characters.

And it was resurrected with the 2008 presidential campaign with both Republicans and Democrats seeing in Barack Obama echoes of the magical Negro, for different ideological reasons, of course. Here is another area where students might object. Be sure your students understand the spirit in which Seitz discusses the president: he hardly condones this characterization of him, just as he hardly condones the character in film and television.

Clearly, this article raises a lot for students to debate and analyze. "Reading the Signs" question 1 is straightforward, asking students to conduct their own reading of how one of the media examples Seitz mentions represents African American characters. For a literary focus, question 4 has students do the same with a Stephen King novel (Seitz calls King's work "a magical negro factory"). To broaden the issue, question 2 challenges students to compare the magical Negro and black domestic stereotypes and argue whether they perpetuate myths about racial identity. One reason Seitz is so passionate about the magical Negro stereotype is its implications for real-life race relations, and these concerns are very real. Thus we ask in question 3 that students address Seitz's contention that changing demographics in America has triggered the current magical Negro resurgence. And in question 5, we ask students to evaluate the stereotype in the context of the even more common stereotype of blacks as violent sociopaths. Here you might get them to consider why African Americans so often figure as either saintly gods or murderous gangsters, and rarely anything in between.

MICHAEL PARENTI

Class and Virtue (p. 361)

Even in the 7th edition, we decided to keep this selection after hearing yet another student proclaim that *Pretty Woman* is her favorite movie of all time. More than twenty years after the release of this film in 1990, it still has ardent young fans, most of whom are female—and, to our surprise, some consider themselves feminists. Although Parenti's writing is direct and accessible, some students are likely to be irked by his position that the film is objectionable on many grounds. He concentrates on the class issues implicit in this film and in others; we've found that many students take class differences at face (read: status quo) value and thus respond to Vivian Ward's transformation by saying, "Well, of course, one has to get of rid of low-class habits." And we've had students argue that the film doesn't really show prostitution because the rich guy is Prince Charming. The film's fans will relish responding to "Reading the Signs" question 2, which invites them to argue with Parenti's interpretation. Be sure your students ask, "Why are we shown *this*?" when offering a counterargument. Parenti mentions briefly the gender bigotry in the film; question 3 sends students to Aaron Devor's essay in Chapter 7 for help in analyzing the film's depiction of gender roles.

Parenti's comments about class can be applied to other media examples. The selection works well when applied to other films such as *Wall Street* or *The Fighter*, or to a TV show such as *The Apprentice* (see question 1); it can also be used to illuminate films such as *On the Waterfront* (see question 4). A more challenging, exploratory topic, question 5 asks students to create a category of "racial bigotry" to parallel Parenti's two categories of class and gender bigotry. For this question, students would benefit by first reading Michael Omi's "In Living Color" (Chapter 7) for a discussion on the ways the media reinforce ethnic biases.

DAVID DENBY

High-School Confidential: Notes on Teen Movies (p. 366)

You should find it easy to get students to talk enthusiastically about David Denby's article, as they tend to love talking about their high school experiences, and Denby's writing is clear, direct, engaging. Ask them if they remember the stereotypical characters Denby describes from their high school days — you'll probably find that they vividly remember such types. Then you can move to a thornier question — To what extent does film reflect reality or shape it? — the question posed by "Reading the Signs" question 4. The stereotypical patterns of the teen social order that Denby discusses have some real cultural implications, especially regarding gender for the target hyper-hormoned audience. Ask your class to consider questions such as the following: What's the significance of the tendency of nerdy male characters to "get" the gorgeous female in the end? At the same time, why do the nerdy girls have to be revealed as secretly beautiful (e.g., they fix their hair properly, start wearing makeup) if they are to get the guy? Students might find it fun and instructive if, in groups, you ask them to plan their own teen movies. Would they rely on the stereotypes Denby describes? If so, why? If not, how would they change the usual depiction of teens?

Denby's article provides a clear framework for analyzing particular films and even TV shows. "Reading the Signs" question 1 has students analyze *The Carrie Diaries, Awkward,* or *90210.* Although the class could brainstorm other current TV programs with teen characters and select an alternative. A more complex topic is posed by question 2, which asks students to assess Denby's insightful, and perhaps threatening, claim that the enemy in teen films is not an adult, but a peer. Question 3 is also challenging, as it asks students whether *The Perks of Being a Wallflower* can be considered a teen movie in Denby's terms. Here, students need to think about whether just having teen characters locates a film in this subgenre.

MICHAEL AGRESTA

How the Western Was Lost (and Why It Matters) (p. 372)

Even Johnny Depp, and a budget of $250 million, couldn't save 2013's *The Lone Ranger* from becoming a box-office flop. So why bother reading about this film? As Michael Agresta argues, the significance of its popular failure extends far beyond the individual film's merits (or lack thereof). Indeed, the western consistently has allowed "filmmakers to explores thorny issues of American history and character," Agresta claims, and with the fall from cinematic favor, he fears, we will be losing a valuable lens on American identity and values. Now some might object that westerns have tended to reproduce some of the more unfortunate sides of American ideology — unbridled conquering of Native Americans, environmental degradation on a large scale, simplistic good versus evil thinking — but that is exactly what Agresta regrets might be lost with the demise of the genre. He points out that other genres, such as superhero movies, tend not to address the larger questions of American history and values. For Agresta, the potential loss of this barometer of American culture is why the fate of the western "matters."

Given Agresta's claim that the western serves as a window on America, a natural essay assignment would be to ask students to do a semiotic reading of any western, whether a John Wayne classic or more modern fare. "Reading the Signs" question 1 solicits students' assessment of Agresta's explanation for why *The Lone Ranger* bombed, while question 2 focuses on the depiction of race in another recent film, such as *Django Unchained* (assigning Michael Omi's selection in Chapter 7 can sharpen students' analysis). Of course, it is not simply the western that offers glimpse of the American mindset; question 3 suggests that students analyze *Avatar* in light of Agresta's selection (they should find many interesting connections, especially when it comes to racial representations). An alternate subject could be a TV show like *The Walking Dead*, which, while not a western, does adapt some narrative tropes from that genre. The most far-reaching question is number 4, which challenges students to argue for their own explanation for what Americans find compelling in film. For this selection, Christine's Folch's selection is an ideal complement, as it offers her own historical explanation for Americans' cinematic tastes.

CHRISTINE FOLCH

Why the West Loves Sci-Fi and Fantasy: A Cultural Explanation (p. 378)

"Oh East is East, and West is West, and never the twain shall meet." Or so Rudyard Kipling wrote with regard to Indian and British cultures. Taking a look from an American perspective a century after Kipling, Christine Folch discovers a striking difference between American and Indian culture when it comes to filmmaking. Noting (as has been remarked throughout this book) a striking preference for fantasy in America, Folch describes Bollywood's preference for the sort of story lines in India that were popular in nineteenth-century British literature: namely, poor boy meets girl, boy gets girl, everyone gets rich. This reading is particularly useful to stimulate discussion not only of cultural difference but also of the ways in which we often take for granted that our current tastes have always been dominant. With a historical approach, Folch provides an interpretation for why Americans today prefer fantasy, and you can begin by making certain that your students understand what her interpretation is. Once you have accomplished that, you can invite your students to offer their own explanations of the current popularity of fantasy in America. This itself can be a useful exercise in seeing how cultural phenomena are overdetermined, which is to say there isn't a single explanation for fantasy's dominance in today's movie marketplace. "Reading the Signs" question 1 asks students to research today's box office favorites and propose their own argument about the popularity of these films. Somewhat simpler, question 2 has students debate the genuinely arguable proposition that American filmmakers are just pandering to adolescent sensibilities in producing fantasy after fantasy. If you'd like your class to address the cultural patterns Folch describes, assign question 3, which asks students to use her essay as a critical framework to analyze a recent Bollywood film. Or you could assign question 4, which calls for a comparison between a domestic-centered Indian film and a movie like *My Big Fat Greek Wedding*, which also focuses on family and interpersonal relations. Here students are likely to discover some decidedly interesting twists on otherwise familiar cinematic motifs.

Chapter 5

THE CLOUD

Semiotics and the New Media

Among the technological innovations that have most influenced modern popular culture — cinema, radio, television, and the Internet — interactive Web-based media have effected a revolution not only in the content and dissemination of popular culture but also in human consciousness. From the user-generated content on sites such as YouTube and Facebook to the multitasking lifestyle made possible by an array of portable devices like the iPhone, iPod, and Blackberry, the shape of popular culture has changed. No longer are popular media in sole control of corporate hierarchies who dictate from above what the content of popular culture will be — a reversal of past patterns within the culture industry that bears significant implications for the future. Your students will have no trouble recognizing the terrain of new media — indeed, they constitute a generation that has grown up within it and knows nothing about a world without it. Their experience with Instagram, Facebook, YouTube, blogging, online gaming — in short, the almost endless array of interactive online media — gives them both an advantage in approaching this topic culturally and semiotically *and* a disadvantage. Their very familiarity may make it difficult for them to realize that things have not always been this way, that our lives are changing in profound ways. They are likely to take the 24/7-communication capability of text messaging and social networking for granted and be unable to imagine a time before cell phones and laptops (even those are a bit passé for some kids). New media represent an enormous change within the historical system of mass culture and mass communication, and getting your students to have a critical awareness of this change may be one of your most important tasks in using this chapter.

Given the ubiquity of new media in most of your students' lives — and the seductive appeal of its functionality in enabling people to communicate — your challenge in covering this topic is to ensure that students maintain a healthy critical distance from the topic. Accordingly, the "Exploring the Signs of the Cloud" boxed question has students analyze their choices in designing a social networking page. Such pages are, of course, elaborate signaling systems in which their creators self-consciously create an identity for the world to see. And often that identity diverges from the flesh-and-blood reality of its creator. To what extent do your students engage in fictionalizing themselves, and why? What sort of community do they hope to attract, and what signs do they use to achieve this purpose? Given the possibilities of fiction writing and the ability to make "friends" with people whom we'll never meet (we deliberately resist using "friend" as a verb), the implications of social networking for ordinary human interaction are profound. "Discussing the Signs of the Cloud" has the class address this matter (such a conversation could well supplement the University of Maryland study on the possible addictive effects of high-tech toys on our students). To broaden students' critical awareness, "Reading the Cloud" has students explore the extent to which user-created content on sites like YouTube may constitute a democratic revolution in media access or, alternatively, is really just more of the same, given that so much such content isn't user created at all, but derives from existing programs and media outlets.

The chapter begins with S. Craig Watkins's essay that explores the ubiquity of "fast entertainment" thanks to our many electronic toys, questioning whether our ability to be "always on" can in fact have damaging effects on our health, social relationships, and consciousness. Even students immersed in all this technology will benefit from Watkins's consideration of how these technologies can shape our lives. This selection is an ideal fit with the next, a press release outlining a University of Maryland study on young people's addiction to media. If you want to address social networking, be sure to assign the chapter's Introduction and the next three selections: danah boyd's essay on how the supposedly revolutionary new media actually replicate the socioeconomic and racial status quo, Simon Dumenco's exploration of why it is so hard to abandon Facebook, and Salvador Rodriguez's lament that social media sites won't let you call it quits, even when in real life you want to quit a floundering relationship. For another focus, the next two readings address ways in which the Internet can bring out the obsessive worst in us, with Richard Rushfield calling for a time-out on instant electronic crowd response to even the most trivial of events and Daniel D'Addario providing a succinct overview of trolling. The concluding essay in this chapter, Henry Jenkins's "Convergence Culture," provides a broad overview of the changes that the new media have wrought on the ways we communicate with each other, consume both entertainment and products, and understand the world.

S. CRAIG WATKINS

Fast Entertainment and Multitasking in an Always-On World (p. 393)

Do you ever get annoyed when your students don't follow your instructions to turn off their electronic devices? Or do you ever get an itch while you're teaching to check your email, but you don't give in to it because you know you'd be setting a horrible example? If so, Watson's essay is for you, because you and your students will relate to his discussion of how the ability to be online all the time is changing human relationships. Indeed, electronic media have created a dramatic shift in both our behavior as consumers, one of the essay's foci, and also our interpersonal relations. As Watkins puts it, "We have evolved from a culture of instant gratification to one of constant gratification," and that desire for instant electronic gratification, whether on a personal, physical, business, or intellectual level, is the theme of his essay

You'll quickly see that most of your students grew up with the assumption of constant media that Watkins discusses. When we've asked our students to report their attention, devotion, or addiction to new media, the vast majority admits to belonging to the last category. One of our students reported in an essay that when she and five friends went out to a nice restaurant for a celebration, the first two hours were devoted to all six bending down to their phones. It was only later that they actually started to converse (and eat). We feel sorry for the servers, but this student's honesty is illuminating. Another confessed to checking his phone for updates at least ten times during each class (yes, sigh). We should add that this notion of addiction applies, to only a slightly lesser extent, to underprivileged students (we both have this population in our classes). Thus you could expect your class to have direct and detailed responses to Watkins's essay.

Our first "Reading the Signs" questions is simple and doesn't require a student to be a new media hog: it asks students' to consider, in their journal entries, the role of being entertained, from whatever source, in their lives. We start this way because so often people today promote being entertained as a high value (as opposed to, say, during the Depression era, when simply living from day to day was the highest value for millions of Americans). Connected to the addiction of electronic media, of course, is the ability to multitask; indeed, instructors often wonder about their students' ability to do that and the possible consequences on their performance in class.

Question 2 confronts students with exactly that issue. For a less personal and more contemplative take on it, see question 3. For essay assignments that bring in more than one reading, try question 4, which neatly pairs Watkins with a University of Maryland research study on the effect of social media on students (see the next essay, "Students Addicted to Social Media"). And for the most challenging question, you might ask students to link the implications of Watkins's essay to Laurence Shames's "The More Factor" in Chapter 1. To what extent is the lust for media/technology/electronics that Watkins explores another variant of Shames's indictment of American popular culture?

INTERNATIONAL CENTER FOR MEDIA AND THE PUBLIC AGENDA

Students Addicted to Social Media (p. 403)

When we first read this article about a University of Maryland research study on the addictive qualities of new media, we instantly knew it would be a perfect addition to *Signs of Life*. Indeed, when our students responded to it in their reading logs, they wrote long, detailed reflections on how they themselves have experienced the addictive symptoms that the article describes. They report that they feel it would be impossible to live without a cell phone; in cases when electronic devices were lost or misplaced, they felt aimless and disoriented; many wish they weren't so dependent on media. Some report that the lure of Facebook is so strong that they deactivate it just before finals week because they don't trust themselves not to use it as a study-avoidance enabler. And others admit to suffering from FOMO: The "fear of missing out" that compels them constantly to check their phones for updates. Students' comments about their news sources are equally striking: most say that they obtain news the same way the University of Maryland study revealed: via social networking sites. As just one example, many had learned about the US raid on Osama bin Laden's compound and his killing via Facebook, Twitter, or some other such technology. So, too, the devastating 2011 earthquake in Japan.

Beyond these personal confessions, of course, are larger issues about the place of social media in our culture, how they affect face-to-face interactions with others, and their addictiveness, although they will not be banned from on high (at least in nontotalitarian nations). And if young people today are getting their news from tweets, what does that say about their likelihood of receiving any information that is even remotely accurate, not to mention comprehensive?

We've found students love to write in response to this article. Our first "Reading the Signs" question calls for the journal entry we've just described. Because students respond so well to this piece, they will likely have a lot to gain from question 2, which has the class conduct their own mini-experiment by refraining from using all of their electronic toys for 24 hours (studying and emergencies can be exempted). To address the matter of reliable news sources, assign question 3; question 4 sends students to S. Craig Watkins's selection for their response to his query about whether media multitasking is "healthy". The last question invites students to research the clinical definition of addiction and write an argument about the term's applicability to reliance on new media. Students are likely to find a host of similarities between substances traditionally considered addictive, such as narcotics, and electronic gizmos — not a perfect fit, but close enough to be, well, sobering.

SIMON DUMENCO

If We're All So Sick of You, Facebook, Why Can't We Quit You? (p. 407)

This selection is a great follow-up to the previous two, especially "Students Addicted to Social Media." If your students find that texting, checking Facebook and Instagram and Pinterest, and everything else they do online proves to be a massive time-sink, they may say, "Well, I'll just take a break from it all for a while." Easier said than done, Dumenco reveals, in this exploration of the business practices that make it nearly impossible to cut the electronic cord to the Zuckerberg empire. These range from the simple—harassing emails that tempt absent users to return—to the more subtly manipulative ploy of convincing you that failure to use Facebook means that you are some sort of social out, an incompetent loser who will fall behind the rest of the crowd. We say this ploy is more "subtle" simply because Facebook doesn't have to be the agent that convinces you that you can't live without it: try logging onto almost any commercial, educational, or business Web site, and you'll find the trusty Facebook link front and center. Indeed, we've found that some ordinary online activities, such as sending an electronic letter to the editor of the *Los Angeles Times*, require a Facebook account.

"Reading the Signs" question 1 asks the class to discuss Dumenco's assumption that "we all love to complain" about Facebook. You could use this discussion as a springboard for an essay assignment about the roles users allow this social media site to play in their lives, both personal and professional. Question 2 prompts students to examine the seeming universality of Facebook use by both individuals and institutions. For this topic, students might survey how one kind of institution (universities, say, or news sources) use Facebook in their operation, then consider the effect of those uses on an ordinary person who might prefer to eschew the opportunity. Question 3 addresses the issue of openness and exclusivity, focusing on Facebook's restrictions on use by nonmembers. Does this policy limit the exchange of information to the public? Or does it largely work to increase the number of Facebook members? Your students will find no easy answers to these questions.

DANAH BOYD

Implications of User Choice: The Cultural Logic of "MySpace or Facebook?" (p. 410)

A pioneering researcher on the cultural and social effects of new media, danah boyd raises challenging questions about the supposedly revolutionary nature of new media on the results of her ethnographic research on media use. She looks specifically at the shift in popularity from the former king of social networking, MySpace, to its successor, Facebook, proposing two different explanations. For one, boyd's interviews show that peers are highly influential: a kid picking a social network site for the first time is likely to go where his or her real-life friends go. And then he or she starts getting virtual friends, and on and on. You'll find that your students will agree with this explanation. However, you might hear many a contrary voice regarding boyd's claims about the racial divisions that she sees in analyzing MySpace and Facebook users. That's fine:

we like articles that offer up a spirited debate among students. She traces Facebook's origins, first at Harvard, and then its migration to other private universities and then further to become the preferred site for most college students. Not so much, though, for ethnic minorities or lower-class kids. Some students reject this argument, possibly because they believe in the romantic notion that technology can be "the great equalizer of society" and possibly because it may not square with their own experience. As one student wrote in her reading log, "It wasn't just my wealthy college-bound friends who changed over to Facebook; it was also my lower-class party friends who chose to abandon MySpace." Others point to the design and aesthetics of the two; as another student wrote, "It marked a transition in attitude, primarily between the immature, rebel stage projected in middle school and the developing maturity experienced in high school as students began to prepare for college and their future. The format of Facebook is simple, elegant, and gives the account users complete control over who they are friends with, what information you want revealed. My neighborhood did not largely consist of students from wealthy families, but almost all students attained a Facebook account regardless of their economic background."

Clearly your students will have a lot to say in response to boyd's argument. As a natural start, "Reading the Signs" question 1 has students explore in their journal their preference of MySpace or Facebook (or no social networking site at all). Interestingly, we've had a few students mention that, in high school, they were social media addicts, but upon entering college, they find the whole matter too much of a time-sink to be worth it. The remaining questions all call for argumentative essays on this topic. Question 2 asks students to contend with boyd's fundamental argument that the choice between MySpace and Facebook replicates the racial divisions in America; for this topic, you might ask the class to interview students from different ethnic and socioeconomic backgrounds about their history with social networking sites. More broadly, question 4 has the class debate boyd's claim that technology reproduces social divisions; the debate can serve as a group brainstorming session for individual student essays on this topic. The film *The Social Network* probably helped to enhance Facebook's success, but it also lends support to boyd's position that the site's Harvard origins contributed to its ability to usurp MySpace's kingship. Question 3 asks students to watch the film and then take on boyd's argument. Finally, question 5 has students study today's version of both sites to determine whether they still bear the cultural and stylistic differences that boyd discusses. As an alternate, you might ask students to compare two other social media sites that are popular today.

SALVADOR RODRIGUEZ

In the Digital Age, Breaking Up Is Hard to Do (p. 415)

If he had read Simon Dumenco's article in this chapter, Salvador Rodriguez probably needn't have experienced so much emotional angst when he broke up with his fiancée, hoping to wipe the slate clean but finding his personal life online all the time. Why? In this brief personal essay written for the *Los Angeles Times*, the technology staff writer laments his inability to electronically exorcise his ex from his life. Although not a profound article, it does raise lots of interesting questions about what "privacy" might mean in the new media era. Rodriguez's goal was simple: after splitting with his fiancée, he hoped to erase all the joint mentions of their former relationship that hovered around in the Cloud. His success was limited; his failures brought him more emotional discomfort than he wanted after going through a painful separation. Some of our students have expressed surprise that it would so difficult to eliminate a former relationship from the Internet; others, when referring to breaking up with a high school friend, could relate to Rodriguez in great detail. Even high school flings live on forever.

This reach of the Internet into one's personal life, even when one moves on, resonates with many students. "Reading the Signs" question 1 challenges the class to brainstorm guidelines for posting personal information online, especially on social media sites. This seems a simple enough question, but it is likely to raise all sorts of thorny problems. You might want to use the class discussion as a jump-start for students' individual essays in which they propose their own guidelines for personal disclosure. A more recent site, Snapchat, claims to avoid the privacy problem by quickly deleting posts. Question 2 asks students to research Snapchat to learn if it indeed lives up to its claims. If not, why not; if so, at what cost to users? For an interview-based topic, see question 3, which asks your students to query others about their habits and reasons for posting personal information. This is a genuinely inductive question; we don't know what your students' results will be, and you should let them know from the get-go that they shouldn't presume a particular outcome as well. If you wish, adopt a scientific model in which students propose a hypothesis; then the results should be interpreted in light of the initial assumptions. For a text-based prompt, consider question 4, which sends students to Rachel Lowry's article in Chapter 7. This selection discusses the ways in which millennials work the Internet to create a personal identity; the question asks students to assume the point of view of one of Lowry's interviews in a letter that offers suggestions to Rodriguez on how to handle his dilemma. Of course, this prompt could be crafted into an essay assignment as well.

RICHARD RUSHFIELD

Toward a Unified Theory of How the Internet Makes Everything Terrible (p. 418)

Does the beginning of this selection's title — "Toward a Unified Theory" — seem off-putting? What about the second part? Probing the connotative disjunction in the title can reveal a lot about Rushfield's point in this blog about our ability to respond to any event online — via Tweets, blogs, social media, you name it — instantly, repeatedly, and unceasingly. On the one hand, Rushfield admits there is nothing really wrong with a community of instant response to a TV show, Super Bowl, late-night show faux pas — and indeed it can recreate bonds among audiences with shared interests. But on the other, he laments the thoughtlessness involved in instant response (thought takes time and careful consideration) and the potential for a kind of mob mentality. And, he notes, in search of ever-higher ratings, networks intentionally push the envelop of incivility and "ham-fisted actions" precisely to generate an instant mob response. He does not provide examples of the latter, so ask your students to brainstorm some: likely responses will be talk shows and reality TV programs. Some students might claim that Rushfield's selection sounds more like a rant than an essay, and their judgment would be accurate. You have a good opportunity here to discuss how and why this selection doesn't seem academic: how would students rewrite it to turn a personal blog into an essay?

Like Daniel D'Addario in the next selection, Rushfield's piece is useful for assignments that challenge students to consider how the Internet has affected our behavior, this time as audience members and fans. The first "Reading the Signs" question sends them to S. Craig Watkins's essay in this chapter for help in analyzing the effect of instant response to online media. Question 2 has them take on one of Rushfield's more trenchant claims about Twitter. What Rushfield describes mirrors the sort of alone-in-a-crowd behavior typical of many a Facebook user who can't bear not to check her wall every two minutes; accordingly, question 3 asks students to consider whether the instant response frenzy can be considered a form of digital addiction. For this topic, the International Center for Media and The Public Agenda articles in this chapter frame the issues perfectly.

DANIEL D'ADDARIO

Everything is "Trolling" Now (p. 420)

When we were kids, we collected trolls, those mushy-faced (and ugly) plastic dolls with a shock of pink or green or purple hair standing straight from the so-called skull. Maybe the word *shock* is appropriate when discussing online trolling, because one of the intentions behind it, of course, is to shock. And to disturb, slander, disrupt. But how did this term come to be used to describe a broad variety of Internet behaviors? Instructors interested in exploring both the Internet and language history will find this a valuable selection to include in their syllabus.

Even before you assign this selection, you might ask your class to freewrite for five minutes, describing what the word *troll* means to them in the context of the Internet and asking them if they have had any personal experiences with online trolling (see "Reading the Signs" question 1). The results can provide a great entrée into this essay, especially if any students relate amusing anecdotes about trolling. But the phenomenon is hardly a mere amusement, of course. You'll want to move to D'Addario discussion of the term's evolution and have the class compare their definitions to what he describes. Where are there areas of overlap? How do the definitions diverge, and why? D'Addario doesn't use the term *flaming*, but it is closely related to trolling. Does your class make a distinction (linguistically, ethically) between the two? It is likely that students are more familiar with incidental trolling — making a comment on a forum just to get someone's goat — and less aware of publications that are considered trolls. Ask them to explain the difference. Ask them as well if they agree with blogger Sadie Doyle's belief that "it's more difficult than accusers think to get people's hackles up." A conversation about these matters can lead the class to a thoughtful consideration of how communicating online differs from face-to-face interactions and how the Internet has shaped our sense of public decorum and civil behavior. The changes in what we consider appropriate conduct provide a good focus for insightful essays.

"Reading the signs" question 2 invites students to weigh the contention that trolling may in fact be positive because it inspires debate and conversation about controversial issues. Because trolling is especially commonplace on politically charged Web sites, question 3 asks students to visit one and study the discursive decorum (or lack thereof) that they observe. They could use their findings as a basis for pondering the extent to which the Internet has changed our basic assumptions about communication. Thanks to the high level of vitriol on the Internet, online newspapers, even the most traditional, have been faced with the dilemma of allowing users to post comments freely or moderating the posts in some way. Question 4 has students prepare their own argument regarding the desirability of such moderation; to develop their ideas, they should survey several online news sites, checking both for any policies regarding posting and analyzing a sample of posts, preferably in response to a charged or controversial topic.

HENRY JENKINS

Convergence Culture (p. 423)

Through four editions of *Signs of Life*, we've included Jenkins's selection for several reasons: Not only is Jenkins a premier academic commentator about the new media and thus a recognized and trusted name on the topic, but his concept of "convergence culture" is spot on and can go a long way in making student enthusiasts of Web 2.0 go beyond celebrating it or, even worse, giving the "what's the big deal" response. Jenkins also is a careful enthusiast who modulates his status as a fan with the recognition that the much-ballyhooed democratization occasioned by convergence culture may not be that at all; it may be more of the usual co-optation by corporate culture of an otherwise individualist phenomenon. Ultimately, he seems to land on the side of the democratization, but his discussion of the corporate hold over this supposedly grassroots cultural shift should give students pause.

Jenkins's writing is clear enough, but his selection does meander some, so you'll want to walk students through it so that they don't overlook some of his key arguments. It opens with a riveting anecdote about a new-media-created Bert-bin Laden clone that illustrates perfectly what Jenkins means by "convergence culture," and he follows with his own definition of the term. You should encourage your students to articulate their own definitions of that concept so that they become fluent with it (and do not simply parrot Jenkins's language). This anecdote is especially potent after the 2011 takedown of bin Laden, thanks to ultra-sophisticated media and technology. After further illustrating what he means by convergence culture, Jenkins complicates it, stressing that it refers not simply to the plethora of technologies out there — a meaning he considers reductive in his description of the "black box fallacy" — but to broader changes in popular culture and human consciousness. These more fundamental changes are the ones students may have trouble grasping, as they may simply take for granted today's convergence culture and the ability to multitask. If your students adopt a "like, duh" response, the University of Maryland's report in this chapter works as a counterpoint, offering compelling evidence on just how convergence technologies have dramatically affected our students' media and social habits.

Students should easily relate to Jenkins's discussion of the many ways new media seep into our daily lives, so "Reading the Signs" question 1 has students reflect on their own experience with new media. This prompt could lay the groundwork for an interesting discussion in which the class catalogues the ways they collectively use new media and when they started doing so. What do your results say about your students' involvement in convergence culture? Do students see any difference between the history of their involvement and that of their younger siblings? What trends do they anticipate for the future? Question 2 invites them to take on Jenkins's somewhat fence-sitting position that participatory media can be either positive or negative; for this topic, the class might first brainstorm recent real-life examples of both beneficial and destructive cases involving social networking sites. For a topic addressing the tension between grassroots participation and corporate control, assign question 3 (the Introduction to this chapter can help further students' thinking on this topic). The ability of individuals to post their own creations on YouTube and similar sites is often romanticized and may be exaggerated, given that so much content is copyrighted material grabbed from other media. Question 4 accordingly has students address the place of copyrighted material on such sites; a strong response to this prompt would include students' canvassing YouTube to evaluate nature of content (to what extent do user-created videos simply show a kid sleeping, for instance, or a more compelling subject?). Discussing in class the "Reading the Cloud" boxed question can help prepare students for this question. A research question, number 5 asks students to explore the ways in which electronic media have been used in recent political uprisings, such as the ones in Egypt and Libya. Can we now take literally the claim that the new media are revolutionary? Have your students decide.

Chapter 6

HEROES AND VILLAINS

Encoding Our Conflicts

In the first five editions of *Signs of Life in the U.S.A.*, we included chapters on real-life or fictional heroes and icons: larger than life figures who embodied our fundamental cultural values. The last few years have not been a very good time for heroes, mythic or otherwise, however, so we dropped that topic in the sixth and seventh editions. But in that time a new cultural dynamic has emerged in American entertainment that has returned the hero, with a difference. That is either through a forceful dialectical relationship with a villainous antagonist (most commonly seen in the superhero storyline) or when the hero incorporates many of the features of the classic villain. This is the antihero, someone we can find in such highly popular TV shows as *Dexter*, *Breaking Bad*, *Mad Men*, and *Sons of Anarchy*. Even the unvarnished villain is coming into mass popularity — as signified in both comic (*Despicable Me*) and tragic (*Game of Thrones*) guises. Although not absolutely new — cinematic and TV heroes have long courted the dark outside (Batman started getting morally complicated in the 1980s, and Butch Cassidy and the Sundance Kid were, after all, bank robbers) — today's heroes and villains tend to tread finer lines of distinction, a muddier moral morass, than in earlier media. And this muddier area extends to real-life signs of heroes and villains. To begin contemplating this muddy area, the "Exploring the Signs of Heroes and Villains" boxed question invites students to compare their favorite fictional and real-life heroes to explore what values they have in common; the question additionally allows for the same consideration of fictional and real-life villains. In both cases, encourage students to look for patterns in their choices.

The emergence of the antihero and the villain offers an excellent opportunity to explore with your students the ways in which popular culture can reflect — and generate — a national mood. From a highly polarized political climate in which one side's heroes are the other's villains, to the increasing moral bewilderment of a society under stress from economic malaise and social change, we can find the attraction of both simplistic hero vs. villain conflicts and the bleak hopelessness of the landscapes of *The Walking Dead* and Westerns. You will want to make it clear such narratives have not always been the most popular story types in American entertainment and that they reflect a profound national disillusionment. Indeed, popularity of villains and antiheroes has become so entrenched that it should make one consider the real-life effects of such tastes in popular culture. The Discussing the Signs of Antiheroes boxed question triggers a class discussion about exactly that, the consequences that may ensue when our entertainment does not simply dramatize but celebrates illegal and psychopathic behavior.

The readings in this chapter move from fiction to reality to demonstrate the social issues at stake when Americans today line up on two sides of a question. Indeed, we see a symbiotic relationship emerging: Is America's increasing political polarization simply being reflected in the media's hyper-creation of villains and heroes? Or is the media's constant pushing of the definitions of villains and heroes encouraging real-life people (citizens, politicians) to act more like their fictional models? The chapter begins with Robert B. Ray's exploration of two hero types in both American history and fiction (the "official hero" and the "outlaw hero"), types that abound not only in mass media but also in real history. While Ray briefly discusses female characters, his focus is largely on men because they constitute the vast majority of fictional heroes. Accordingly, his selection can also serve as a useful frame for discussing the gendered nature of heroism in the mass media, especially when read along with the next selection by Stevie St. John on the evolving character of Wonder Woman. A set of paired readings follows that explores the villain and the antihero variant that is so prevalent today: Heather Havrilesky explains why viewers do not simply tolerate, but enjoy, horrible bad guys such as Walter White and Donald Draper, and Laura Bennett then questions the very utility of the word "antihero." The next two selections provide a twist on the notion of heroes and villains, as George Packer studies how today's celebrities have become a new "superclass" that thrives on the widening gap between the rich and everyone else, and Noah Gittell explores how corrupt business executives have become a favorite Hollywood villain in a time when the daily news is filled with reports about real-life corrupt business executives. Focusing exclusively on real-life individuals, Tim Layden's "A Patriot's Tale" tells the story of real-life heroes that just about everyone could agree on in the immediate aftermath of the 9/11 attacks on the World Trade Center. To explore the notion of heroes in greater depth, the "Reading Heroes Online" boxed question has students analyze Internet lists of historical heroes: students question the criteria used to create such lists and determine what values underlie them. An interesting twist would be to compare two such lists and to examine the differences between them. Concluding the chapter, Lorraine Devon Wilke's "Snowden's a Hero, Obama's a Villain" demonstrates just how messy things have gotten more than a dozen years later, with America's political antagonisms forming some often surprising alliances.

ROBERT B. RAY

The Thematic Paradigm (p. 450)

Ray's selection has been one of the most frequently assigned in the earlier editions of this text—and that's no surprise. It's useful no matter what films your class analyzes, and whether or not you emphasize semiotics, because it focuses on two essential patterns of protagonists in American films: the outlaw and the official hero. That is why we have moved this selection to lead off our new chapter on heroes and villains, because Ray's critical framework encompasses the topics raised here fully.

The outlaw/official hero dichotomy is by no means limited to Westerns, as the terms might suggest. Your students can find these protagonists in action-adventure, mystery, political, and even romance movies. Ray thus provides a clear, accessible paradigm for interpreting characters from almost any film. Students should have little trouble identifying the paradigm, but be sure to review the ideological significance of the two character types—a more abstract point that students may overlook. Ask, for instance, why Americans tend to prefer the outlaw hero. What does that reveal about the American character? To encourage students to consider the significance of Ray's categories, we strongly suggest that you assign "Reading the Signs" question 2, which asks the class to brainstorm examples of outlaw and official heroes, then to categorize them according to shared traits (such as race or gender).

Ray's selection provides an ideal framework for analyzing not only films but also other media. Questions 1 and 3 are similar, asking students to apply Ray's paradigm to the central characters in *The Hunger Games* and *Sons of Anarchy*, respectively. Question 4 is speculative, asking students to create a third category of hero to accommodate the characters in such cartoons as *The Simpsons* and *South Park*. The last question also asks students to extend the range of Ray's analysis, inviting them to explore the applicability of Ray's categories to female characters.

STEVIE ST. JOHN

Out of Character: Wonder Woman's Strength Is Her Compassion—What Happened? (p. 459)

With the traditional hero being a male warrior, the cartoon superhero followed in kind, until the advent of Wonder Woman and a host of female superheroes. But consistent with conventional gender codes, Wonder Woman has generally had a kinder, gentler inflection than her male compatriots—and has also gotten a lot less cinematic attention, as Stevie St. John observes in her analysis of comic book history's "longest running female superhero." This reading will, accordingly, present your class with an opportunity to explore the gendered side of heroism. If you have the class respond to the "Reading Heroes Online" boxed question, which asks students to study online registers of historical heroes, you can have them explore the possible real-life origins of the gender-coding of heroes: What percentage of the heroes that they find are women? And what activities constitute their heroic actions? What relation do students see between the historical lists and the gendered patterns in fictional superheroes?

This selection is ideal for prompts that focus on either gender or the notion of heroism itself. For straightforward assignments that call for an analysis of female superhero characters, try "Reading the Signs" question 1, which asks students to compare Wonder Woman with another female superhero, or question 4, which sends them to Aaron Devor's "Gender Role Behavior and Attitudes" in Chapter 7 for help in analyzing the gender codes implicit in Wonder Woman's character. (A more nuanced version of question 1 would add Devor's framework to the comparison of the two characters.) For a creative exercise also focused on gender, assign question 5, which challenges students to adopt Mariah Burton Nelson's perspective in "I Won. I'm Sorry" (Chapter 7) in an analysis of the traditional gender roles that female superheroes typically embrace. Although athletes are, strictly speaking, not superheroes, the media often portray them as such (especially men), and Nelson's exploration of the mixed social signals conveyed to women athletes dovetails with St. John's discussion of Wonder Woman's character.

If you prefer that your students consider the notion of heroism, assign question 2, which invites them to analyze Wonder Woman in terms of Robert B. Ray's official/outlaw hero dichotomy. Note that we do not assume that Wonder Woman would neatly fit either category, and your students should not feel obliged simply to slot the character into one. The most challenging question is number 3, which asks them to explore cartoonist Phil Jimenez's claim that popular culture changed after the 9/11 terrorist attacks, with superheroes given more license to engage in violent pursuit of ever-more evil villains. This claim raises the question of how popular culture serves as a sign of political attitudes. To buttress their responses to this question, students should ground their essays in a close analysis of specific TV shows or films. You might also find it useful for the class to read the Introduction to Chapter 4, particularly the reading of *Batman: The Dark Knight*, for a sample analysis that locates its subject in the context of the 9/11 attacks.

HEATHER HAVRILESKY

No Sympathy for the Devil (p. 465)

Why is it that TV audiences have flocked to programs about truly evil and hateful protagonists? And why do some such shows fail and others succeed wildly? Havrilesky's selection offers an insight response to such questions by focusing on two hits, *Breaking*

Bad and *Mad Men* (although cancelled, both were recent and popular enough that your students are likely to be know them quite well). It's important that your students recognize that Havrilesky isn't simply talking about "bad guys"; she is analyzing characters that aren't "supposed to be lovable," who go beyond the pale in their unethical behavior, simply beyond redemption. Indeed, you might pause and ask what she means by "redemption," as that is the crux of her argument. The class might make a list of TV bad guys and consider which, if any, are redemptive. The selection itself can help with identifying such distinctions, as it is framed as a comparison between *Breaking Bad/Mad Men* and *The Sopranos*, a show with an unquestionably criminal and deviant protagonist whose willingness to reveal his vulnerabilities earns him redemptive status, at least in Havrilesky's view. Or maybe students believe that Tony Soprano deserves to be categorized along with Walter White and Don Draper? These questions have no easy answers and thus should trigger a lively conversation about what American audiences find likeable, appealing, or appalling in their most-watched TV protagonists.

You'll find it easy to devise essay assignments that can apply to a wide range of TV programs (and, of course, films, if you prefer). "Reading the Signs" question 1 essentially calls for students to probe what Havrilesky means by "the likability" of protagonists (her understanding of that term is only implicit in the article). You might have the class discuss their definition of this term, keeping in mind this selection; that conversation can be a starting point for students' individual essays in which they define what makes a character "likeable" and test that definition on a particular protagonist from a show of their choice. Also implicit in this selection are definitions of *hero* and *antihero*; accordingly, question 2 invites students to do a close reading of "No Sympathy for the Devil" and articulate the assumptions Havrilesky makes about those terms. Reading the Robert Ray and Laura Bennett articles in this chapter can help lead students to more nuanced arguments. Question 3 has students write their own analysis of one of the three shows Havrilesky discusses; their essays could be stand-alone analyses or could support or take issue with the selection. The broadest question is the fourth, which has the class brainstorm current TV programs that feature antiheroes; this class list could form the foundation of an essay in which students write their own argument about why antiheroes have become so popular. In what ways is their popularity a sign of the times? How do they signal America's current cultural and political mood? To develop their ideas, students would benefit from reading the other essays on heroes and antiheroes in this chapter, along with the chapter Introduction.

LAURA BENNETT

Against Antiheroes (p. 471)

While there is usually a subtle, but significant, distinction between trends and fads, when it comes to the antihero there is no such distinction at all. In short, the antihero trend in American culture is also a fad, and Laura Bennett's exasperated reaction to the way that everyone seems to be talking about antiheroes these days in one way or another shows how a significant cultural trend can be trivialized through overexposure into sheer meaninglessness. So a good place to begin with this reading is to ask your class if they can think of any other faddish trend that doesn't really mean anything anymore (such as wearing baseball caps backward). Why do people perpetuate the trend? Do they even know it has been a trend?

Of course, you also will want to discuss Bennett's argument about the term *antihero*. To what extent do they find it valid? You might test her claims on a reading that uses the term, such as Heather Havrilesky's "No Sympathy for the Devil" or the Introduction to this chapter. Is it the case that the term "barely means anything at all," as Bennett claims? "The sheer volume of antihero references" in the media bugs her: Do your students think that is simply because writers have glommed onto a trendy word, or could it be that the many references are evidence that more antiheroes populate film and television? Given the tenuous nature of Bennett's position, this selection invites essays that assess it. "Reading the Signs" question 1 asks students to evaluate Bennett's claim that "antihero" is overused; to support their argument, they might survey recent film and/or TV reviews and determine for themselves when and how the word appears. Taking a somewhat different approach, question 2 asks students to read one of the texts Bennett indicts for overusing "antihero" and to assess the validity of her critique. If the reason the word is overused is because antiheroes abound in literature and popular culture, they may indeed simply be a familiar archetype. Question 3 sends students to Linda Seger's selection in Chapter 5 to tackle the question of whether the antihero is an enduring character type that speaks to the human psyche.

GEORGE PACKER

Celebrating Inequality (p. 474)

One of the most morally complex of human figures who could, from one angle at least, be regarded as a hero is the celebrity, and any section on heroes will certainly benefit from an exploration of that peculiar invention of modern mass media. George Packer's take on the celebrity is especially useful for such a study because he adopts a historical approach to the topic while offering a distinctly ethical point of view. In brief, for Packer the contemporary celebrity is little more than a villain who, in an era of ever-diminishing opportunity for anyone but the one percent, casts a shadow that starves the rest of us of needed economic sunlight. Eliciting your students' personal reactions to this demonization of people who may be their heroes would be a very lively, and certainly provocative, place to begin with this reading. They might not mind Packer's dig at Kim Kardashian, but some will have qualms about debunking Mark Zuckerberg or Jay-Z.

You should be sure that your students are all on the same page when using the terms "heroes" and "celebrities" and that they understand how Packer uses these terms. "Reading the Signs" question 1 suggests that the class discuss these terms (ask about both their denotative and connotative meanings); that conversation will prepare students to write an essay arguing for their own definition of these words. The next questions challenge students to address what today's cult of celebrity reveals about American values and ideologies, with question 2 focused on the place of fame in our culture and question 3 calling for a response to Packer's belief that the American myth of opportunity has disappeared. For a research topic, see question 4, which has students study the public relations surrounding one of the celebrities Packer mentions and assess his charge that "they live by the hacker's code." For a prompt that starts with introspection, question 5 has students write in their journal about their favorite celebrities and why they have earned that status; these ruminations could lead to an essay in which they subject their favorites to Packer's critique of celebrities. The results may indeed be eye opening.

NOAH GITTELL

The Lone Ranger *Seals It: America's New Favorite Villain is a Rich Guy (p. 477)*

Yes, you might wonder why *Signs of Life* has two articles on *The Lone Ranger*, given that it wasn't a successful movie. But be careful about reading titles too quickly: this selection is much more about American class ideology than it is about the film. How so? *The Lone Ranger* is really Gittell's jumping-off point for his exploration of how recent movies have turned business head-honchos into today's archvillains. He moves from that film to two films of different genres, *Iron Man 3* and *White House Down*, to suggest that *The Lone Ranger* is not an outlier in portraying corporate types as the bad guys. Moreover, he specifically identifies greedy capitalists as the cause of war (his argument is more subtle than his title suggests). In the process, Gittell is proposing a cultural trend that reveals much about American values and concerns. *That* should be a focus of your class discussion. You might have the class brainstorm recent cases of corporate malfeasance and controversies over the conduct of the war on terror. How have these events created a climate ripe for films with this "new favorite villain"?

Beyond essays that agree or disagree with Gittell, this selection is ideal for prompts that can trigger highly nuanced arguments. "Reading the Signs" question 1 asks students to compare Gittell's treatment of the Western with that of Michael Agresta in "How the Western Was Lost — and Why It Matters" (Chapter 5); they should recognize that both authors consider the Western as something of a Rorschach test of American values and beliefs. As noted above, Gittell bases his claims on three different film genres, a strategic move to broaden the applicability of his argument. For a textual analysis, assign question 2, which solicits students' evaluation of this argumentative move. For a semiotic analysis, try question 3, which has students interpret the protagonist of *The Wolf of Wall Street*. Although this film does not have a link to war, it fits the bill of presenting "American business interests" as anything but heroic.

TIM LAYDEN

A Patriot's Tale (p. 481)

We have brought this reading back from the fourth edition of *Signs of Life in the U.S.A.*, which we were working on that fateful day when the World Trade Center towers were destroyed and the world itself changed. Today there is something poignant in the uncomplicated heroism of the first responders who climbed the tower stairs to save lives, only to have the skyscrapers themselves fall down on top of them, a poignancy made sharper by the later fate of Pat Tillman, who signed up for military service in the spirit of those New York City firefighters, only to be killed by friendly fire in Afghanistan. And oh, what a mess we face today, as the two wars America fought since — in Afghanistan and Iraq — appear to be devolving into futility and failure. Plenty of villains to go around, but heroes are harder to find.

It is the historical *difference* that forms a good place to begin your discussion of this reading. Most of your students will be too young to have clear memories of

September 11, 2001, and the days immediately after, when Americans from across the political spectrum flew Old Glory and purchased thousands of action figure toys modeled on members on the New York City Fire Department — when Rudy Guiliani was still a hero unbesmirched by allegations that he mishandled the crisis and its immediate aftermath. For a brief time, much of America came together: Ask your students if they can detect any such unity today. And ask them about whom they might consider heroes, like the 9/11 first responders, who forgot about self in order to serve others. And how deeply do we regard our heroes? Such questions combine, in "Reading the Signs" question 1, a contemplative prompt that has students explore Americans' regard for their heroes. Lorraine Devon Wilke's selection in this chapter can help them develop their ideas; if you wish, you might add an interview component to this question. That would be most effective if students were to query people of different ages about their devotion to heroes and how it may have changed over time. One reason we include "A Patriot's Tale" is because the heroes are "ordinary" people doing "ordinary" work in circumstances anything but ordinary. How often do we consider regular folks heroes, as opposed to the famous or the rich? Question 2 has students explore the criteria we use to define a hero by first having the class brainstorm their own choices of hero. Then students should analyze the results, looking for patterns in the criteria that the class has used. (Tip: If you keep an electronic record of your students' brainstormed heroes, they can refer to it at home when they are drafting their essay.) Something of a capstone, question 3 calls for a comparison of real-life and fictional heroes: What distinguishes them? Do they share any common traits? For this prompt, students could draw upon any of the readings in this chapter, along with the Introduction.

LORRAINE DEVON WILKE

Snowden's a Hero, Obama's a Villain (p. 486)

On the day we are writing this sentence, a national poll has just declared Barack Obama to be the least popular president (or, to be precise, the "worst president") of the post–World War II era. Now, whether this poll has any validity is not the point; what does matter is the long way Barack Obama has come from the days of the Shepard Fairey "Hope" poster and the Nobel Peace Prize. And we're not talking about right-wing abuse here: Obama, once a hero to millions of liberal-leaning millennials, has lost his heroic status and, particularly thanks to the NSA scandal, can be a villain to many who once adored him.

What makes Lorraine Devon Wilke's consideration of the matter so useful is the fact that she has no patience for such clear-cut, black-or-white judgments. The real problem, Wilke believes, is the American tendency to see *everything* in childishly oversimplified ways — "arrogant" and "entitled" she calls it. The world comes in shades of gray, she argues, and it's high time we noticed that. Any discussion in your class of the NSA scandal or Obama or the Tea Party or most any current political topic should begin with a clarification of the much larger point about American culture as a whole that Wilke is making here. Be prepared for some discomfort in your students, however, because the tendency to see things in righteously oversimplified ways is so pervasive an American trait that it might be included among our fundamental mythologies.

Wilke's exhortation to abandon binary thinking and "to be willing to see past the black and white" is ideal for a writing course, as most instructors push their students to recognize shades of gray, subtle nuances in argument, and the like. "Reading the Signs" question 1 invites the class to discuss writing strategies that would satisfy Wilke's plea; for a follow-up exercise, it has students evaluate an op-ed piece from a newspaper or other media source. Much the same work is the focus of question 2, but this time students should focus on Wilke's article (interestingly, some bloggers responded to this Huffington Post piece by criticizing the author for black-and-white thinking). Some students may wish to address the actual political circumstances that Wilke discusses, so question 3 allows them to write their own evaluation of the Edward Snowden affair (or perhaps another controversial issue). To consider a contrary view, question 4 poses the proposition that seeing the world in grays can be dangerous, inviting a moral relativism and lack of intellectual and ethnical commitment. (Ironically, we think the better responses to this question would indeed recognize more than fifty shades of gray!) The last question leads students to the world of black-and-white thinking, as it has the class list criteria for being a political "hero" or "villain," then asks students to analyze a current topic that invites binary thought. The Fox News/MSNBC split would be a good place to start!

Chapter 7

MY SELFIE, MY SELF

Ma(s)king Identity in the New Millennium

Whether the result of a postmodern resistance to rigid classifications, or the outcome of decades of multicultural education and feminist illumination, we've noticed that contemporary students often resist social categorizations based on race or gender. With a growing population of mixed-race individuals, America itself is entering a new era wherein traditional demographic categories are appearing less and less relevant. This tendency has been especially enhanced at a time when an entire generation of millennials is engaging in intensive online self-profiling, whether for personal or professional reasons, with one high-profile outcome being Facebook's designation of some 56 (at last count) gender identities for its users. For this reason we have maintained our combination from the seventh edition of *Signs of Life in the U.S.A.* of what in previous editions had been separate chapters on race and gender into a single chapter, reflecting thereby not a dismissal of the relevance of race and gender in everyday life and popular culture, but instead a recognition of their new, more flexible configurations.

And thus we see this chapter as something of a capstone to the entire book. Identity has long been explored in writing classes and composition texts, of course, and that topic typically is introduced in the beginning of a course and early in the course's accompanying reader. And we understand, and indeed have ourselves taught, with that sequential logic. Nonetheless, increasingly we see that asking students to address their identity with narrative or personal essays, maybe a critical article or two, can leave them in the prewriting space of journals and reading logs. Accordingly, we intend this chapter's placement in this edition of *Signs of Life* to lead students, through a combination of induction and deduction, to a deep understanding of how cultural codes and mythologies have shaped their sense of personal identity. Indeed, in our recent restructuring of our own classes, we see students writing their best about identity issues *after* they have examined the ways in which advertising, commercial culture, and popular entertainment have influenced them before they arrived in their college comp class.

Hence, the organization of the chapter. We start with a discussion of online self-profiling and its potential confusions, because this experience is probably the most immediately relevant to your students. Several readings devoted to gender identity follow, in line with a cultural tendency that *Time* magazine in 2014 described as having reached a "tipping point": a movement toward a widespread recognition of transgendered identities. The readings on gender begin with a paired set that addresses the nature/nurture debate surrounding gender roles. Aaron Devor explicates how gender is socially constructed; Deborah Blum then counters his position by outlining the ways in which biology affects gender roles and behavior. When we assign these readings, we typically ask students to contemplate in their reading logs what shaped their own notions of gender when they were growing up, and they usually attribute their assumptions to both biological and social influences, including media. Because Devor and Blum focus on heterosexual gender roles, to counter the equation between gender and heterosexuality we include next Kevin Jennings's poignant memoir about growing up gay and coming to terms with his sexual orientation. Focusing on women athletes, Mariah Burton Nelson follows with her lament about the professional straightjackets that traditional gender norms place on us.

We do not ignore more traditional identity classifications such as race and class, for in spite of more fluid and experimental attitudes toward gender identity, race and class continue to be trenchant and (regretfully) divisive forces in American life. Class has actually become of heightened importance given the era of Occupy Wall Street and a growing gap between the rich and everyone else in America, so we especially recommend Alfred Lubrano's reflections on class identity as it affects college students.

Race, particularly, has always been a critical component of American society, but many social changes — for instance, successes in the civil rights movement, a political and legal backlash against those successes, increased immigration from non-European nations, and increased opposition to such immigration — have heightened Americans' sensitivity to race and racial conflict in recent years. Thus Michael Omi's essay is essential because he provides a broad theoretical overview of racial attitudes and explores how those attitudes are manifested in popular culture. The chapter concludes with three selections that illustrate how complex indeed the very notion of personal identity has become.

A few words about using these readings in class are in order. Discussing multicultural issues can be tricky, especially if your campus has experienced racial tensions or if your students come from ethnic backgrounds that historically have been at odds with each other. The potential for in-class conflict is not a reason to avoid the topic; in fact, it's probably the most compelling reason to address it. Students' ability to succeed in school may depend, in part, on their ability to handle those kinds of conflicts, and their writing class may be the only structured environment in which they can explore them. You'll find that semiotic analysis is an optimal way to handle class discussion of race because, rather than focusing on private passions about the topic, it addresses the way race serves as a sign for the culture at large and for one's own sense of self. Indeed, in the Introduction to this chapter, we deliberately ask "Who are you?" to suggest the potency of race in shaping one's personal identity. But even when working on a personal level, a semiotic approach links the individual's views with those of the system, the larger society. The emphasis, in other words, is on the cultural mythologies about ethnicity that shape our sense of self and our worldviews. To go beyond the personal, you can assign your students the "Reading Identity Online" question, which asks students to visit Web sites devoted to the culture of a particular ethnicity, gender, or social subgroup in order to analyze the breadth of information available. You might want your students to share their findings in class, so they can assemble a composite description of the Internet sources they have found. In addition, the "Discussing the Signs of Race" boxed question asks the class to consider the profile of an American demographic that will soon have no majority race: What are the possible consequences?

Much the same can be said about the chapter's second focus, as gender is also a part of our identity that has biological roots shaped by cultural and social codes. We've found that students usually enjoy discussing gender issues and considering their own assumptions about gender and how these assumptions were formed. In our experience, it's most effective to structure class discussion to stimulate lively but controlled conversation about these issues. You can alternate between arranging students in same- and mixed-sex groups, for instance, to take advantage of gender dynamics. You might want to do that with the "Exploring the Signs of Gender" question, which asks students to contemplate in their journals or reading logs the ways their upbringing affected their notions of gender identity. If you have an ethnically diverse group, asking students to contribute perspectives that differ from traditional American gender norms can help show how they are culturally, not biologically, constructed. Note that we selected our readings on gender to show students that gender is a topic for both women and men. Occasionally, male students quietly tune out when class discussion turns to gender, assuming that they are not "marked" by gender, as are their female peers. We wish to counter that assumption, for we believe males and females, heterosexuals and homosexuals, are equally subject to our culture's gender norms and mythologies, though the effects can differ radically for each group and for each individual.

RACHEL LOWRY

Straddling Online and Offline Profiles, Millennials Search for Identity (p. 500)

We've found our students to be galvanized by this opening selection, as Rachel Lowry's discussion of how millennials struggling to create a personal identity explores how the online world makes what has always been a difficult transition to adulthood even more complicated. In this article for the *Deseret News*, Lowry addresses several dilemmas that young adults face. One emerges when they go on the job market and find that their prospective employers have already screened them on Facebook or LinkedIn, and the applicant doesn't really know how much the interviewer knows about his or her private life. Another comes from the pressure to join social network sites — one woman whom Lowry interviewed feels she has no choice but to appear on social networks as she's job hunting — and then deciding what sort of identity to design. Given the competitive job market, many feel tempted to engage in self-promotion, which often can translate into exaggeration or deception. As Lowry points out, it's hard to reconcile the "real" identity with the online persona. Your students might not yet be on the job market, but they are likely to connect with the dilemma this selection describes. Ask them about their online profiles: How have they chosen to present themselves to the world? To what extent did they craft a persona to appeal to a particular sort of visitor? Did they enjoy or resist the idea of "self-branding"?

Such a conversation will prime students for writing about the effects of social media on their sense of personal identity. "Reading the Signs" question 1 calls for a journal response to students' own profiles on social media (or if they do not participate, why they have chosen not to do so). The next two questions address the pressures and complications that social media have occasioned, with question 2 focusing on the ways it has affected the job application process and question 3 weighing the relative influence of adults and peers on one's social media behavior. The most open-ended prompt, question 4, asks students to synthesize the selections by Salvador Rodriguez and the International Center for Media and the Public Agenda, and to create their own argument about how social media affect millennials' sense of identity. For a more ambitious version, students might additionally interview some young social media users about their experiences. Students might also find Thomas Hine's essay on packaging in Chapter 1 — particularly the packaging of personal identity — additionally useful.

AARON DEVOR

Gender Role Behaviors and Attitudes (p. 504)

We highly recommend that you include Aaron Devor's essay in your syllabus, for its overview of gender roles and the signs used to communicate them provides a strong critical framework for discussing gender identity. Note that Devor's writing style is somewhat academic, so the selection can also be an occasion for discussing critical reading strategies and techniques for comprehending academic writing. You might ask your students to annotate the essay as they read it, and then, in small groups, to review their annotations as well as their sense of what Devor's major points are. Or ask them to prepare review questions. At the beginning of class, have students write their questions on the board; you can quickly see which parts of the essay may have been confusing and thus warrant in-depth discussion.

Despite the academic style, Devor's essay is well worth the effort. Not only does he chart the traditional cues of "masculinity" and "femininity," he makes clear how they are cultural constructs, not biological necessities. You'll want to make sure students understand that, when talking about these cues, Devor is describing social norms, not his recommendations for how people should act (we've had a few students complain that he wants women to be passive — quite the contrary). His emphasis on the social construction of gender thus makes the essay a must-read if you're using a semiotic approach. Students tend not to dispute his general claims about socially construction, but they do occasionally balk at two of his premises. Some may resist the notion that signs of masculinity carry with them a position of social power and dominance — in other words, that gender norms can have some inequitable consequences. And some may be discomforted by Devor's suggestions about mixing gender norms (the selection is excerpted from his book *Gender Blending*). It could be useful to broaden the terms of discussion to include the presumption that heterosexuality is the "normal" sexual orientation in America, but be prepared to hear some reservations on this matter.

Because Devor provides a broad theoretical framework for viewing gender identity, this selection is ideal for applying to specific evidence. Consider doing the first "Reading the Signs" question in class before discussing the essay; that way you'll be able to refer back to students' assumptions about gender later. The question asks students to brainstorm gender traits in small groups and then to write their lists on the board. If students form same-sex groups, we can guarantee a lively discussion! Even students challenged by Devor's essay should be able to respond to the remaining questions. Question 2 has students assume the role of sociologist by asking them to use their friends' behavior as evidence they should analyze in terms of gender norms. Question 3 picks up on Devor's comments about body language and sends students to popular magazines to examine the gender-related postures of models (we've found that men, in particular, are allowed a limited range of postures in ads, with the limitations being greatest in men's magazines such as *GQ*). The Steve Craig selection in Chapter 2 can help deepen students' analysis. Finally, question 4 asks students to address the genuinely debatable issue of whether fashion continues to restrict the female body more than the male body.

DEBORAH BLUM

The Gender Blur: Where Does Biology End and Society Take Over? (p. 511)

As a clear explication of biology's influence on gender behaviors, Deborah Blum's piece serves as a direct counterpoint to Aaron Devor's claim that gender is a social construct. As Blum herself points out, her argument is not exactly politically correct (readers familiar with the work of writers such as Emily Martin will bristle at her acceptance of the term "default sex" in reference to females). But her viewpoint is not reactionary: We like her essay precisely because it avoids the simplistic either–or thinking that often dominates the culture vs. nature debate on gender matters. Indeed, Blum acknowledges that many of our gender codes are cultural constructs; what she argues, however, is that evidence suggests that biology has far more influence on gender behaviors than most humanists want to admit. To academics accustomed to social construction theories, her position might seem untenable, but another reason we like this piece is her careful approach to argumentation. In a nice Rogerian style, she begins with a personal anecdote that validates her readers' likely assumptions that gender is only a social construct (this piece originally appeared in the *Utne Reader*) and then explains how her thinking about gender evolved to include biological influence. Ask your students to chart the many ways in which she anticipates her readership's probable responses to her claims. Even though Blum occasionally talks about XX and XY chromosomes and Leydig cell hypoplasia, she is a Pulitzer Prize–winning science writer who knows how to make technical information accessible to the nonspecialist reader. You can use her piece as a model of clarity and specificity.

We've found that students tend to enjoy discussing their own upbringing and how their notions of gender norms developed. Indeed, because they often are quite open about the topic, their own experiences are a good starting place for class discussion (see "Reading the Signs" question 1). Particularly if you pair this selection with the Aaron Devor essay, your students should be well equipped to write argumentative essays. The natural question to accompany this pairing is "Reading the Signs" question 2, which invites students to respond to Blum's challenge to the social construction view of gender. Because Blum talks a good deal about her own observations as a mother, students may want to discuss child-rearing strategies; an imaginative topic, Question 3 prompts students to suggest appropriate ways to raise boys or girls to avoid stereotypical behavior, given the biological evidence that Blum sets forth. To extend Blum's argument, question 4 invites students to research the current findings on the genetic basis of sexual orientation (recent studies have found that homosexuality may have some genetic origins). We encourage you to study in class the photo of the American Girl doll store opening on page 515. Ask your students: Who are these stores designed to appeal to? What is the photographer trying to say by including a line-up of similar-looking doll faces? What, if anything, does this photograph suggest about the origins of gendered behavior? For a textual analysis assignment, see question 5, which sends students to Lorraine Devon Wilke's selection in Chapter 6 for a critical framework for analyzing Blum's argumentative strategies.

KEVIN JENNINGS

American Dreams (p. 519)

Kevin Jennings's selection is one of our favorites, and not simply for its clear writing, mild humor, and engaging individual voice. In this personal narrative, Jennings describes how he came to terms with being gay while growing up, combating not only normative gender roles but also his own sense of insecurity. In the process, Jennings creates a whole cultural context for understanding why gays and lesbians are so often seen as the "other" in our society. Indeed, as he describes his growing desires during adolescence to join the mainstream, to capture the traditional American dream, what emerges are multiple layers of "otherness." First Jennings became aware of geographical otherness and attempted to erase the signs that he was a Southerner. What's interesting here is that he became an active participant in maintaining the distinction between mainstream and other. What's even more interesting is that Jennings repeats this pattern, for a time, with his sexual orientation. That is, initially he tried to deny his homosexuality to himself, and this effort continued even when Jennings got to college. Note that when

Jennings says that by accepting his identity as a gay man he has "done the most American thing of all," he is assuming a different definition of the American dream than the one he assumed in the beginning of the selection. Be sure to ask your students how the dream changes for Jennings throughout his process of self-discovery.

Although some students may find Jennings to be a tad sentimental, most will respond positively to this very open piece. Given the personal nature of this selection, students may enjoy responding to "Reading the Signs" question 1, a journal topic that has them reflect on the pressures of normative gender roles that they may have felt during their teens. For a challenging argumentative topic, try question 2, which addresses the tendency of some minority groups to erase their identity, or question 3, which focuses on popular media's role in perpetuating a heterosexual norm. For a research topic, see question 4, which asks students to research the current status of same-sex marriage and to write an argument about the extent to which Jennings' plea for unqualified equality for gays and lesbians has been realized. Note: As we write this in July 2014, 19 states and the District of Columbia allow some version of same-sex marriage. It would be interesting to see if this number has changed when you assign this article to your class!

MARIAH BURTON NELSON

I Won. I'm Sorry. (p. 524)

Here's a reading that will be especially poignant to your women students, especially if they are athletes. As Mariah Burton Nelson makes clear in this selection, the codes governing our gender roles can exert many contradictory pressures, often in unexpected ways. In particular, she focuses on the dual roles that female athletes must play: On the one hand, they need to be tough and aggressive in order to succeed in their sport, but on the other hand they are expected to be feminine and submissive, especially around male athletes. And as she points out, it's not easy to be simultaneously passive and aggressive, charming and ruthless.

Your students will have no trouble with Nelson's accessible and clear writing, but be prepared for some defensiveness when it comes to her questioning of the beauty demands that women athletes face, because Nelson strikes at the very heart of the conflicting gender codes that govern the world of sports. Your students may prefer women athletes who, despite defying convention by entering what is traditionally regarded as a man's world, still abide by the old gender rules by muting their competitive drives and, so to speak, putting on high heels. So expect some comments to the effect of "What's wrong with a female athlete's desire to look pretty?" You can remind students that, in a semiotic analysis, your goal is not to judge right and wrong, but rather to investigate the ideologies and assumptions underlying cultural practices. You might ask your students about a complementary contradiction involved in the Dove "Real Beauty" ad campaign: As Jennifer Pozner's article in Chapter 2 discusses, the campaign has been controversial for the mixed messages in using "ordinary" women to sell products to make them more beautiful. And you can extend the discussion to men: Are there arenas in which men face parallel contradictory gender codes?

"Reading the Signs" questions 1, 3, and 4 are all assignments that call for an argumentative essay in response Nelson's contentions about the dual gender codes that affect female athletes. By asking them to observe some women athletes in action (question 1), to analyze a women's sports magazine (question 3), or to interview women athletes on their campus about the gender pressures they face (question 4), you will not only be guiding them to a sound basis for assessing Nelson's argument but also helping them to appreciate the value of empirical evidence. Question 2 suggests a personal and reflective exercise, which may be especially valued by female athletes who themselves face the conflicting pressures that Nelson describes.

ALFRED LUBRANO

The Shock of Education: How College Corrupts (p. 531)

Your students may find the title of this selection to be, well, shocking. How can education be "shocking"? How can it "corrupt" anyone? When they read Lubrano's selection, however, most will find that they can easily relate to his tale of the "status dissonance" occasioned when a blue-collar kid leaves a rather drab home life for the bigger, faster, cooler college world. This essay, based partly on personal experience and partly on Lubrano's research, relates moving tales of families and relationships torn apart by the conflicting values and personal styles found at home and at school. Lubrano's term for such students is *straddlers*, people who are on the move from one class to another and find that "home" no longer fits them very well. He first outlines his own experience as a student at Columbia University, finding the need to "self-censor." You can ask your students: What are the values that are in conflict, and how does Lubrano handle the strain? Do you think he could have used any alternative strategies to cope with familial divide? If they think that Lubrano is making much ado about nothing, have them consider his characterization of the way middle-class students "are groomed for another life" in the selection's second half. How does that experience differ from the working-class upbringing he describes, and why does that difference grant middle-class kids some advantages he doesn't have? The conflicts extend beyond family to relationships, and students may well connect with the tale of Loretta Stec, whose relationship with her construction-worker boyfriend became increasingly strained when she went to college. Even those students from wealthier backgrounds are likely to respond to the tale of two sweethearts growing apart with the distance of miles and experiences.

That is true as well of the family strains created by a student being immersed in a different world, one with more worldly and intellectual values than that of mom and dad. Although students from working-class backgrounds are most likely to be living the conflicts Lubrano describes, students from any background may be feeling that learning, and just being at school, is separating them from their families and old friends. We find that students love to talk about their own experiences as students, their struggles to adapt to college. Thus "Reading the Signs" question 1 is a journal topic that encourages students to reflect on any changes they perceive in their connections with family and friends. This topic can allow you to gauge their reactions to being in college—especially helpful with first-year students. A creative twist on this topic would be to adopt the perspective of Lubrano's mother and to write him a letter about her response to the family conflicts occasioned by his college attendance. But Lubrano's essay allows for more than personal responses. An argumentative question 2 asks students to support or refute the claim that learning creates a gap between parents and children; you can allow your students to use personal experience and their observations of others as support. This prompt can also trigger some field research in which students interview their contemporaries, preferably from a range of backgrounds, about whether they have had to adjust to college in the ways that Lubrano describes. A textually focused essay is triggered by question 3, which calls for a synthesis of the three personal accounts that Lubrano describes. Question 4 triggers the most ambitious assignment, which has students assess Lubrano's assumption that working-class students face conflicts with their families that more advantaged students tend not to experience. We suggest students work inductively by interviewing students from a range of classes, then synthesizing their results into a coherent argument. Finally, question 5 calls for an analysis of Lubrano's use of evidence, quotations, and sources. Ask students to study which voices are quoted directly and which indirectly. Do they see any class implications in the patterns they discern? This question prompts a careful exercise in close reading and observation.

MICHAEL OMI

In Living Color: Race and American Culture (p. 538)

We've kept Omi's essay through to the eighth edition both for its clear exposition of the prevailing racial beliefs in America and the influence of those ideas on the formation of personal identity, and its focus on how those beliefs are manifested in popular culture. It is thus one of the more important selections in *Signs of Life* because of its critical framework for analyzing the way race, as expressed in popular culture, can affect one's self-identity. Students should find Omi challenging but accessible. He doesn't use the word *semiotics*, but essentially he provides a semiotic reading of race and racial images. His underlying assumption is that cultural myths about race are socially constructed but are seen as natural categories. Race and racism are, of course, sensitive issues, but Omi's article is useful because he focuses on the process whereby ideas about race are created, rather than evaluating individuals who believe the ideas. In class, be sure to discuss the central concepts he advances for talking about race: overt and inferential racism; unexamined racial beliefs; the ideology of difference, or otherness; situation context; and invisibility. While Omi defines these concepts, the terms are probably foreign to students.

The essay lends itself to assignments extending and complicating Omi's analysis of the racial images that prevail in American popular culture. We highly recommend "Reading the Signs" question 1, which asks the class to brainstorm common racial stereotypes and then to discuss how these stereotypes are perpetuated in popular culture. If students have difficulty doing the second task, you might organize their discussion by medium (e.g., advertising, movies, etc.) so that they can more easily focus on particular examples. You can use this discussion to speculate on the media's power to shape our understanding of the world and even our own racial identities. What difference does it make, for instance, if movies consistently depict gang members as black? What's wrong if advertising presents Asian students as hardworking and industrious? Don't be surprised if someone responds, "But isn't that true?" Such a question, of course, corroborates Omi's claims; you might invite other members of the class to respond. The remaining topics allow students to examine racial imagery and assumptions in various aspects of popular culture. Question 2 has them explore how films such as *12 Years a Slave* or *My Family/Mi Familia* may affect American attitudes toward racial identity. Students can have some fun responding to question 3, which asks them to analyze ethnicity in a magazine targeted to a specific ethnic readership. We suggest that you have students work in teams so they can share their insights, or ask students to present their findings to the class. Question 4 has students test one of Omi's major claims on a film or TV show of their own choosing. For this one, the class might brainstorm examples that would be good candidates for analysis and then choose a limited list that students can watch (so you can specify broadcast dates and won't need to view two dozen programs). Because *Avatar* presents a particularly rich and complicated array of racial representations, question 5 asks students to focus their analysis on this film.

DANI MCCLAIN

Being "Masculine of Center" While Black (p. 550)

The possible permutations of personal identity become particularly complicated when two or more traditional categories, like race and gender, are involved. In the case of Dani McClain's journalistic report on black women who adopt "masculine of center" identities, the result can be a certain amount of conflict. Being what might be called "cisracial" (that is, identifying with their birth race), such women who choose transgendered identities can find themselves threatened within their own demographic communities as well as outside of them. Black "trans men" face similar conflicts in a world where conservative attitudes toward transgenderism are shared among all races.

In short, this reading may provoke a certain amount of emotion among your students, especially if you teach in an environment that is hostile to transgendered people. If you anticipate such a reaction, first discussing Aaron Devor's and Deborah Blum's articles in this chapter could be useful, because the former's explication of social construction can lead students to see how often assumptions about gender are normative, and the latter reveals the biological imperatives that guide our understanding of our own gender identity. While masculine of center women are not necessarily trans, they certainly do not fit commonly recognizable groups. Indeed, you might want to ask your class to explore the very term *masculine of center*. What are its connotations? When students first heard or read the term, what assumptions did they make? The focus of "Reading the Signs" question 1, these queries could trigger both a lively class discussion and a challenging essay on linguistic specificity. For a broader overview, see question 2, which asks students to contemplate Facebook's fifty-plus categories of gender identification. Where would the women featured in McClain's essay fit? Students should use their particular observations to form a more comprehensive argument about the ways we define gender identity. Whatever your students' attitudes toward alternate gender identities, they are likely to be struck by the fact that the women who deviate from the norm meet not simply surprise from others, but outright hostility and violence. Question 3 solicits students' arguments for why women who adopt unconventional gender identities face such a violent response. While Mariah Burton Nelson discusses a rather different (and decidedly more conventional) group of women who are not conven-[illegible]nal — female athletes — she also reports the hostile response many receive, and [illegible] her selection can usefully broaden the issues for students. For another prompt [illegible] addresses violence, question 4 asks students to research why LGBTQ people of [illegible] are even more susceptible to physical violence than their white counterparts.

Students should use their findings as the basis for an essay in which they argue how and why social norms may drive some people to extreme, not to mention illegal, actions. To develop their ideas, student might visit the campus LGBTQ for further history and information on violence against those who march to a different gender drummer.

THERESA CELEBRAN JONES

Sanjay and Craig: *Nickelodeon's Hilarious New Mixed-Race Heroes (p. 554)*

When most Americans think of mixed-race identities, they usually think in terms of African and European unions, but, of course, the burgeoning numbers of mixed-race Americans include individuals with some combination of Native American, Asian, South Asian, Hispanic, and/or European ancestry, which is what makes Theresa Celebran Jones's celebration of the mixed-race cartoon *Sanjay and Craig* especially useful. Centered on a boy whose father is Indian (i.e., South Asian) and mother is European (white), *Sanjay and Craig* belongs to a growing number of children's television programs that feature not only mixed-race characters but also immigrants from parts of the world that have traditionally received little attention in American popular culture.

Because Jones's brief reading is frankly grateful to Nickelodeon for creating such a program, you might want to explore with your class the tone of her essay. Is Jones simply lauding *Sanjay and Craig*, or does she go a bit further than that? We think the latter, but the brevity of the piece might mask the fact that she isn't simply calling for more mixed-race characters; her bottom-line desire is that our culture reach the point where such characters are no big deal, just part of the norm. Do ask your students about whether they forecast such a future in American TV, whether in kids' cartoons or other sorts of programming. Why or why not? Jones also finds it significant that the show's producers are white. Do your students get why she finds that detail important?

You can assign a number of fun, engaging, yet serious, assignments based on this essay. "Reading the Signs" question 1 is direct, asking students to argue with, support, or modify Jones's reading of *Sanjay and Craig*. If their reading is significantly different (we don't predict difference or similarity), you might prompt them to compare earlier episodes with later ones and to analyze the possible causes of the differences. One of Jones's foci is racial identity, of course; a tougher essay prompt is question 2, which sends students to Jessica Hagedorn's selection in Chapter 4 to glean insights on stereotypical depictions of Asians characters. Even though Sanjay is of mixed race, does he display any of the clichés about Asians that Hagedorn exposes? A broader version of this focus on racial identity is the theme of question 3, which asks students to assess the representation of race in the context of mass media overall. For this prompt, it would be most effective if students were to locate *Sanjay and Craig* in the most relevant context — children's programming, especially cartoons. Otherwise, students might be overwhelmed and inadvertently compare not only apples with oranges but, worse, smartphones with manatees.

AYMAR JEAN CHRISTIAN

The End of Post-Identity Television (p. 556)

For many Americans, the election of Barack Obama in 2008 signaled the beginning of a "post-racial" era, a revolutionary cultural shift that, as Aymar Jean Christian suggests in this blog, was anticipated by a spate of "post-identity" television programs in the early 2000s in which the characters' race or the sexuality of the characters were not of any particular concern. Considering this submersion of cultural difference, Christian takes the reemergence of identity television as a welcome sign that identity (as cultural difference) still "matters," even as he suggests that the post-identity era was based on a counterproductive "myth." Why? His response is pragmatic: real politics.

Christian provides an excellent opportunity to discuss with your students their own attitudes toward cultural difference as well as the current trend toward flexibility when it comes to questions of personal identity. For Christian, race, gender, and sexuality are relatively fixed categories. Do your students agree? You might move from that general discussion to a more precise definition of what Christian means by "post-identity" television. That term should not be taken literally: TV characters still have marked identities (otherwise they wouldn't be defined characters — problematic for TV). But how are they so marked? Your students can test their understanding of this concept when they respond to "Reading the Signs" question 1, which asks them to respond to Christian's assumption that the mass media largely have entered a "post-identity" phase. In their essays, students should be sure to ground their general observations on details drawn from specific TV programs of the moment. For a more focused question, assign the second, which sends students to Jane Hu's selection in Chapter 3 for a close analysis of *Girls*. Christian's article suggests that many post-identity TV shows feature black characters who are then slighted by critics and viewers alike; question 3 challenges students to explain this pattern (Michael Omi's selection in this chapter can provide them with a useful critical framework). Question 4 shifts the discussion quite a bit as it turns to David Denby's selection in Chapter 4 on teen flicks; students can analyze whether today's teen movies — which, as Denby suggests, tend to repeat convention after convention — have arrived at the post-identity phase. As a capstone, the fifth question asks students to consider whether America has indeed become a post-identity nation. For this one, students could engage any of the readings in this chapter (and the Introduction); the readings pointing toward the representation of race, ethnicity, and identity in chapters throughout the book could also be foundational texts.

Missing something? Instructors may assign the online materials that accompany this text. For access to them, visit **macmillanhighered.com/signsoflife8e**.

Inside LaunchPad Solo for *Signs of Life in the USA*

Tutorials

Critical Reading

Active Reading Skills

Reading Visuals: Purpose

Reading Visuals: Audience

Documentation and Working with Sources

Do I Need to Cite That?

How to Cite an Article in MLA Style

How to Cite a Book in MLA Style

How to Cite a Database in MLA Style

How to Cite a Database in APA Style

How to Cite a Web Site in MLA Style

How to Cite a Web Site in APA Style

Digital Writing

Photo Editing Basics with GIMP

Audio Editing with Audacity

Presentations

Word Processing

Online Research Tools

Job Search/Personal Branding

LearningCurve

Critical Reading

Topic Sentences and Supporting Details

Topics and Main Ideas

Working with Sources (MLA)

Working with Sources (APA)

Commas

Fragments

Run-Ons and Comma Splices

Active and Passive Voice

Appropriate Language

Subject-Verb Agreement

E-readings

Gene Brockhoff, *Shop 'Til You Drop* [DOCUMENTARY FILM CLIP]

Ford Motor Company, *Two-Ford Freedom* [VINTAGE ADVERTISEMENT]

The Beverly Hillbillies, Getting Settled [TV EPISODE]

Louis J. Gasnier and Arthur Hoerl, *Reefer Madness* [FILM CLIP]

George A. Romero and John A. Russo, *Night of the Living Dead* [FILM CLIP]

Nancy Schwartzman and Isaac Mathes, *xoxosms* [DOCUMENTARY FILM TRAILER]

U.S. Immigration and Customs Enforcement, *iGuardians* [VIDEO]

Sut Jhally, *The Codes of Gender* [DOCUMENTARY FILM CLIP]